Frogs and Fuckeries

BY

CHELSEA BLACK

Frogs and Fuckeries

Chelseablack.net

First printed in the United Kingdom, 2021

Published by Conscious Dreams Publishing
www.consciousdreamspublishing.com

Edited by Rhoda Molife
IG: *@molahmedia.com*

Typeset by Oksana Kosovan

ISBN: 978-1-913674-41-0

To Stephen

Table of Contents

PART 1

The Challenge Is Set

The German Awakening

I woke up in a German hotel next to a 70-something year-old bright orange-haired woman feeling like I'd died. Note – it wasn't ginger it was orange. I think she was going for red though.

She told me about my antics the night before which involved me asking my new friend if he was gay (to be fair his current FwB – Friends with Benefits was quite masculine-looking), going home with a guy from the Congo and lap dancing halfway across a bar. I'd like to blame the meds and the alcohol and the birthday I'd just celebrated but let's be honest, it was mainly alcohol and being in Germany. This was a combination I will never repeat as I just don't like Germany. The alcohol? I can't make any promises.

Let's go back…

After years of attempting to date organically I was an older, wearier blogger who wrote about the things that happened in my life and assumed that someone, anyone, would read it. This was to prevent the recycling of the same old stories to the same old seven friends who worriedly asked about my life and tentatively wondered why I was still single? I had become somewhat lazy and bored of the same endings. Yet again, a man I dated or talked to wasn't the one. Oh why couldn't there just be a shoe that I could take around the clubs of London like in *Cinderella*? I mean, many men wore a wide size 12 (this could be total wishful thinking on my #sizequeen part when the average shoe size was actually a 9/10).

Blogging meant that I didn't have to reiterate the woes of living a modern life. Yes, dramatic, but most bloggers are, right? Let's accept and move on. I was bored of dating misadventures and wanted more than waking up next to a woman and throwing up for 24 hours with alcohol poisoning. I wanted a relationship like everyone else wanted. A companion through this shit thing called life. Prince had just died, and we were facing a referendum on Brexit, so I was feeling particularly philosophical and pessimistic at this point. What better way to distract myself than with a relationship?

Then one day, I got to thinking and realised that to be perfectly honest, bloggers probably say very little about themselves as they're always too busy bitching about experiences, services, products and, in my case, dating frogs. Just know that I find the science of retelling my dating experiences as the cheapest form of therapy I can afford. I can't pay someone to listen to me going through yet another optimistic attempt at meeting someone. I can't. I won't. I don't have the budget.

That's where you come in. Hello, my singirls and singuys! This is the second book in what I hope is a short series because dating is rather time consuming and tiring. I don't want this to turn into an American version of what was a perfectly great UK TV series like they did *The Office or Queer as Folk*. Short and sweet is how I like it. The first book, *Cupid's Cockups* was a post-divorce memoir of almost dating, dating disaster rants and is my random dating and sexual exploration across London. At the time, I was under the illusion that I would trip upon a penis and be out of the dating circus within months. This didn't happen. It has now been years. I have slowly accepted that I may be stuck here for a while. This is now like those '80s TV show where every episode is about escaping and yet, somehow the heroine or hero ends up in the same place by the end of the season. Was my 'season 2' going to break the mould?

I decided that I needed to step out of passive dating and actually *do* something about it. This 'mizz-adventure' sees a more mature me taking a more structured approach to dating in commemoration of ten years of post-divorce dating and knowledge. What did I learn, I hear you ask? Honestly, I learned that the internet had ruined dating and that men were still celebrating not having to pay on dates to get sex anymore. I learned that there were a lot of damaged souls out there looking for someone to project all their issues onto. I learned that society and education have failed a whole generation of men and, subsequently, women. All of this in a strictly *cis* – hetero-normative way of course. I'm hoping everyone else is having a much better time of things than single, Black women in London. That about sums it up. If you choose to stop reading at this spoiler alert, then I won't be upset. I'm pretty disappointed too. However, there were some gems in the mud I must add and some glimmers of hope.

Some woeful wastemen will try to linger past their expiry date but for the purposes of this book, we will ignore any feeble attempts at a comeback. There is no space for any 'Return of the Mack' attempts. We will not have it. This isn't Upper Street (please google the boy band Upper Street if this reference makes no sense to you. They were an attempt to take members of previous boybands and create a super band). I'm sure you've realised by now that you will need the aid of the internet to read this book because I am not be a millennial and my references are safely positioned in the pre-millennial era. I sort of lost the will to bother with keeping up with modern day references after *Big Brother* Season 2.

Some dates were cool as in we quickly figured we did not want the same things. Like, it's great that you're really into Scientology but I'm not on Tinder to change my religion. I mean, not all of them were trying to be arseholes. Some were angry, others sad, a few depressed and some just going through a shit time. The dating recession clearly didn't discriminate. The majority were really wasteman though, navigating this modern dating world like the worst of them do. I do sort of see them as angels, demons, ghosts and ghouls. So this quest to slay is apt.

What is a wasteman you ask?

A wasteman is a man who wastes your time because he's not serious about you and/or his life. His life philosophy centers on his 'base need' which is not to be tied down by any woman and his 'ego need' which is to be adored and looked after by women. He is a free sexual spirit. He will give you the impression that he wants to be tamed but this draws you into a false sense of hope and feeds into your need for a potential project. It's a lie. Don't fall for it. No man needs a woman to coach him into maturing and getting into a relationship. You are not strong enough my singirls. He will ghost you and you will wonder why. It's part of his DNA, and for you that means, do not answer his calls.

Generally, he's found living at home or renting with others during his late 30s and up to his 60s before the council put him into care. And they're not just domestic beings. The 'travelling wasteman' also exists. He will claim to be a laptop millionaire through something called affiliate marketing but gets western unions from the Bank of Mum and Dad or the ghosts of girlfriends' past. He just couch-surfs or finds a woman at the club who will adopt him so that he can move out of the hostel.

He's a 'slasher' who has time to go to the gym and look cute. Slashers tend to have five different job roles all of which make no money except the one in retail or fast food or bars. The rest are simply great slasher fillers, e.g., rapper, artist or philosopher with no real body of work or need for money. Then there are the rapper-slash-barista-slash-political activists on hash-tagged causes. He will not normally be defined by one role unless he is a musician or poet. Alternatively, he may be an overgrown student with four degrees, all pending completion or payment or work experience.

He can usually sex well because the quality of his sex determines whether he gets a home-cooked meal and a bed for nights on end when there are too many people at the house-share or Mum has church group. I call them '*hobo-sexual*' as they do whatever they need to do to maintain a roof over their heads and get fed. Another skill of his is ghosting or tagging you while keeping your 'non-relationship' going for years on half-whispered promises and a bit of cunnilingus.

He likes to do some or all of the following: hang with the guys, drink, do drugs he didn't buy, daydream, draw, waste people's time, pretend he's 15 years younger than he is and headfuck you, both literally and emotionally. Why is he a headfuck? Because you spend all of your time trying to work out why things aren't working before you eventually realise that it's really him and not you. But the most dangerous thing of all is that a wasteman is a parasitic being who lives to suck the life out of others while searching for the perfect home to call his own without having to do very much. Beware. This creature lurks heavy on internet dating sites and apps. And hence the fuckeries one gets from frogs.

Some may see this as one woman's rants and ask, 'Well, what's wrong with her?' The answer is that, apart from some weird eating habits, a love of '80s music and gay kindle books and a habit of giving the benefit of the doubt, I'm quite alright. Not an 8 or even a 7.7 but a strong 6.5/7 out of 10. So, dating shouldn't be this bloody hard. But then I may have to just accept this concept of a dating recession. More on that later...

Just to clarify being single is a perfect way to explore this world. I love it. If anything, to give up one's single status is one of the biggest decisions a woman has to make and one that shouldn't be made lightly. That's one of the biggest lessons I've learned since *Cupid's Cockups* to now, what I call *Frogs and Fuckeries,* though the title may lead you to believe that I haven't learnt much.

Now truth be told, we have to consider where society is right now. We are facing political regression and societal upheaval as the internet exposes people's insecurities and real musings. Instagram selfies are a pet peeve as I walk around London trying to avoid statues of idiots taking shots of... themselves. The COVID19 pandemic has added another layer of complexity with video dating and socially distanced walks taking the place of quick meetups. But this was before all that... before the world imploded.

Read on and see, enjoy and here's to hoping we all live happily ever after.

Chelsea Black 2021

Dating Resolutions

So let me take you back to the very beginning…

Every year I go through the same behavioural pattern which suggests that I will get the same results, right? Not in my stuffing-filled brain. *Side note*: I love stuffing but only the overly processed Paxo sage and onion which I suspect doesn't have onions in it as I detest onions. Add a little unidentified sausage meat and you're laughing all the way to the Sunday roast dinner slumber. I digress. You're going to have to keep me focussed, which leads me back to the purpose of this challenge.

And so I start to panic after a particularly hectic year and scribble down some fanciful but totally unachievable resolutions for the following year. Yes, my name is Chelsea Black and I'm one of those terrible people who flood social media with tales of things I'm going to do every year. Sometimes I manage about 3 of the 12. Mostly I just stop posting about it and hope that nobody notices. To be honest, nobody ever does so we're good.

I love to plan weight loss, a new job, new love and a whole new attitude and yet find myself two weeks in back on the sugar and moaning incessantly about how shit everything is from dating to my work situation. "This is going to be our year," we cry until Valentine's Day when we realise that once again, we are spending it at a singles speed dating event in Stoke Newington wondering when everyone decided to grow a beard and hide their smiles (read smiles as lies). I hate beards almost as much as I do onions. I'm pre-hipster and millennials and *BuzzFeed*. To me, beard are basically vagina bushes on self-conscious, trendy guys' faces. I much rather you bare all and I can see how pock-marked your skin is from years of neglect instead of you scratching my soft skin with that wiry beard. You know what's a turn on for me? Knowing just how hard you have lived.

This year was different as I fell ill with flu on NYE. Not the best time as I was midway through hosting a NYE party and all I wanted to do was chuck everyone out and crawl into my soft blankets and sleep. Even my blankets felt itchy. By 2am I was over everybody, the red sequinned dress was irritating my skin and I couldn't drink. Not in the way I wanted to see in the new year. Nobody needs to see that shit in sober. Nobody.

I only had five goals for this year. This was a massive improvement from the 12 I usually set. Yes, I know it's not original to have one for each month, but one has to keep oneself motivated, no? So these were my five:

Married – Yes, I know that this is my goal every year and, to be clear, it's not about a pea mint themed wedding. It's about finding my soul mate and enjoying our pea mint themed wedding photos on a regular basis. Shit! What if he hates pea mint? Urgh! I'll have to rethink themes. Even my resolutions were themed 'M'. This was already stressing me out.

Making babies – See married. I'm ready to ruin my body for some bundles of joy. My body wasn't ever that much of a priority to be honest and at least I'd have someone to blame. Mrs Arthur, the P.E. teacher from 20 years ago is off the hook.

Marathon – To be honest, after the last one I only keep signing up for another as a means to staying slim. I don't think this is the right sort of motivation, but I was determined to do another.

Master French – I chuckle writing this as I freeze whenever anyone talks to me in French and still think it's relatively alien even with subtitles. But this year I was going to do more. Or talk about doing more again. French is hard.

Money – To be able to give up #WorkWoes and just live a life of relative bliss.

Matchmaker – To become like a Black Patti Stanger with plenty of Black love couples living happily ever after.

I was nought-for-five and then realised that there were six. Well, I did manage to match a few couples, but apart from that I got a severe case of writer's block, my dating disasters reached peak levels of pathetic ergo, there was no baby making and I cried tears of joy when the email from London Marathon saying I hadn't got a ballot place landed in my inbox. I was grateful to get my lie-ins back.

How Dating Has Lost Its Sparkle and Shine

So there is such a thing as not being able to get a date for love or money. I'm currently in such a 'phase' of the dating cycle. In actual fact, it's a dating recession.

A dating recession is a sign of the times. OK. I will stop with the references to songs by Prince but to be fair his death was such a shock and I'm still in mourning. Whilst it's fine to accept that the whole world is going through this phase, what it means is that it leaves a whole bunch of women stuck in the crack between '90s RnB love songs and Hollywood rom-coms. Headfuck here stands for happily ever after dating fuckeries because the reality is that men and women don't always want the same thing and it all starts off with that long, drawn out passive-aggressive fight also known as the first date.

During the height of *Cupid's Cockups,* I easily had five to six dates a week and I was riding the dating high with tales galore and a wardrobe to match. This was before the need to post every single outfit on Instagram or Facebook. Seriously, how many times would one want to be seen in the same LBD (Little Black Dress)? OK some of them were NSA (No Strings Attached) dates but they count too, right? Don't judge. It's not cute.

But then the dating bubble burst and now I'm in negative dating equity. My friends are starting to say it's me. Words like, 'too picky' are being bandied around with careless abandon whilst none of them are offering anyone from their backup crew. You know, the five guys most women have that they could get with if pressed but don't because it wouldn't work out for long? Men also have backup crews too. They call them friends they fuck.

How is it that this year I've only managed to have *one* date and that one was based on my spending hundreds on plane tickets and warm clothing? This isn't a life; this isn't how dating is supposed to be!

Back in the day we were giddy on dating. Now you think twice before you leave your house. I don't understand it. My male friends tell me that they don't want a drinks date to turn into a dinner date. It's too expensive. Huh? Is this dating recession completely financial or is there more to this phenomenon than meets the eye? OK maybe we should first examine the financials, then the other possibilities, before we make any conclusions.

Finances

I get it, you don't want to waste money on a full-on dinner. And God forbid if she's a drinker. That bottle of wine can quickly turn into two. Yes, yes, the average woman does the reach for her purse but, if you are old skool, you wouldn't dream of letting her pay for it. That's sarcasm by the way.

In my case, I seem to be asked out a lot by men whose wallets detach from them more often than not, but for those that don't, why would you really resent paying for a dinner date? Is it because deep down you still think that dating is a transactional relationship in which sex is paid for? I would check what dating really means to you as I have no problem buying dinner for a new friend or colleague. So why should dating be any different? Besides, you can dictate where you go for dinner and make sure that it's within your budget.

TMI Too Early

Exhaustion

Maybe you could just be tired. Dating is stressful and after a while it does start to feel like hard work. No more butterflies and frantic calls to friends asking what you should wear. Instead, it's fitting it in between work and episodes of your latest boxset. You may have dating burnout in which case take a break and come back to it later. Don't force it. Nobody wants a reluctant date.

Time Wasters

I hate being interviewed but having dated aplenty, I quickly know whether someone is worth bothering with. Friends and my mother will say give them more of a chance but, when it's a no, it's a no, right? The most recent date I had went on and on about himself on the phone and didn't seem interested in me at all. I'm already time poor as it is and don't have time for wastemen. Most of us don't want to date. We just want to end up in a relationship with the least drama possible.

Unfortunately for men, women still want the courtship thing, so this lack of emotional seduction often doesn't work. I don't want a guy who is all too comfortable spending time in my flat but doesn't think going out and exploring the city is important. Right there, our values already differ.

So check yourself during your dating recession. Yes, there are a lot of options out there but by now you should know what's important to you and what you want out of dating. Maybe you're burnt out and do need a break or maybe you're still living like it's 2008 when the recession was hard. Get yourself a Taste Card or a Nando's card. You won't regret it. Keep looking, stay positive and that right house, I mean, person will come along. There are ways to do this dating thing so that it doesn't break you or your spirit, right?

My Last First Date Theory

When a woman says no to penis she is labelled as 'too fussy'. It's a dick. One is allowed to decline. Sigh #40DayDating #Frenemies"

Dating is a curiosity and there is no boundary to the questions asked of daters. When it comes to dating, people seem to care for two obvious reasons:

1. You're single and are dating and going through the same shit as me or,
2. You're in a relationship and want to smugly laugh at the dating perils we singletons must go through in this modern age.

Either way, I can tell you that as unlikeable as I may seem (apparently, I can come across as finickity and a dating snob) and as bad as some of the dates were, we have to be able to laugh and have hope. Hope because every date we take is one date closer to the last first date, the last first kiss, the last anxiety-fuelled drama date. Yay! This is my terribly cynical and yet hopeful theory for dating. I'm now kissing less frogs as I get closer to meeting 'the one'. Or 'the three'. Let's not discount polyandry as an option.

Dating Update Since Cupid's Cockups

So, I've been on this dating journey before. Back then, it was less structured, and I spent most of the time finding myself in random interactions with a seedier part of the population. I would like to blame all men for this but, the truth is I was post-divorce and exploring what I really wanted out of life. *Cupid's Cockups* was in no way a means to finding a partner for life. Yes, I tripped over what I thought were some princes along the way (I somehow managed to get engaged twice without rings so I'm not sure if they properly count. Would the Council of Engaged Women deny my application to join their club? I guess we'll never know), but they just turned out to be toads. I'm mixing up my metaphors, but you get where I'm going. This dating fairy-tale isn't easy at all. The quest for love involves more misery than merry men in tights. I was over the worst of a 'happy-ever-after' mindset and was more focused on finding someone I could tolerate for more than a meal to hang out with.

Since *Cupid's Cockups,* I had a few revelations brought on by life events. The first was that I had been assaulted several times and dating wasn't fun anymore. Being assaulted usually means that you ask yourself what you were wearing and what did I do to provoke him.

Apparently, I had turned up and I ate. Guys thought a Nando's and some banter meant that they could take without asking. Nah. I'd also gone to therapy and that had me thinking about why I did half the stuff I did. I will say this, when you meet a great therapist then you will love talking about yourself for 50 minutes every week. My sessions lasted for 16 weeks which was just long enough to focus on the issues without feeling rushed. I loved it.

Lastly, last year, I was diagnosed with a chronic illness which meant that I'd taken stock of where I was in life and what I wanted. This sense of focus was new to me as generally the only thing that made me focus was sugar. So having ill health for the first time ever made me re-think how I spent my energy and made use of my time. My illness also meant that I had to battle restaurants for gluten-free food every day. We all have a struggle, I guess. This was to be mine.

Whilst I wanted to date and meet someone, I wasn't going to shag anyone just because they had a big dick or dressed or smelt really nice. Ok, I didn't think this thought out loud, but I did think I should stop being overly impressed by a £40 bottle of aftershave and some decent deodorant. Notice I don't mention the big dick. If a guy is gifted, then I say we celebrate that even if he's got a few flaws. Let's just say that this took me a while to put into action. I didn't say I was totally fixed yet, right?

So here I was being forced to change how I dated and interacted with men. The first thing that went was my flirting. I know! I felt bereft but there was a reason. Inadvertently, I had become this incorrigible flirt which put sex at the forefront of my interactions. This was fine when that's what I wanted but some men didn't get that this wasn't a cue for sex. Just flirting. So after the second (or was it third) sexual assault I just switched off. I lost my *joie de vivre* in a way and despite trying, I couldn't get it back.

Secondly, I wasn't going to have sex until I was in a relationship. Another first as most of my relationships developed from sex. I know, some of us do things in a topsy-turvy kinda way. Now it was simply that I didn't have the energy to go clubbing and bar-hopping anymore. Besides, my illness also meant I had to stop drinking. There is only so much water a woman can drink without peeing every 40 minutes (that's three glasses by the way). So naturally, I had to switch to apps and online because I'm somewhat lazy and am always on my phone. It made sense from a statistical perspective, right?

So I decided on a self-made 40-day dating challenge. Yes, I know that should have been the name of the book but *Frogs and Fuckeries* sounded more authentic. It was a 40-day challenge because I was intent on breaking old dating habits which never lasted long. I was nearly as determined to break these habits as I was to find myself a man.

I chose 40 days because I'd done so many 30-day challenges only to fall back into old habits afterwards. In my mind 40 was a sweet spot. I didn't research that bit so don't sue me if you try it and it doesn't work for you. We are all just trying to find a solution to the old age need to find someone to share our happiness with. I was going to actively date and treat it like a full-time job instead of something I did on the side.

I also thought that it would be nice to say that despite so much evidence to the contrary, there are great men out there; men who want the same things that women want and don't feel the need to disrespect, lie, cheat or headfuck anyone to get it. Naïve perhaps, but I can't live not believing that the Universe created me and therefore it would have created somebody out there to explore life with me. Somebody who thinks the perfect date is eating and laughing and chatting about music and books and Marvel and the sadness that is the Black British music industry or the demise of Labour and the Liberal Democrats. The simple life is all one seeks. Nothing more. No emotional games or baggage that seeks fixing.

It seemed simple enough right?

Happy Birthday to Me

I was so on focus and was going to make this the best year *ever*. I could blame Brexit (still not over the complacency) and Trump (the world will never, ever learn from past mistakes). Instead, I carried on with my weekly French class and pretended that the marathon was still happening.

I needed to get my arse in gear and get on this dating thing hard. It was now May and still no luck. I had to rethink my whole strategy if I hoped to ever get married and have babies. Running was beginning to feel like work, and I couldn't find my trainers. Let's face it, I was going to have to settle at being plump.

So late the night of my birthday party, I signed back onto Tinder and Plenty of Fish – PoF. I was going to date for 40 days and give love a chance. Bestie and I giggled over profiles and cooed over others. Some were just so damn outrageous that we wanted to slap them. Instead, I swiped left (To the left, to the left, everything you don't want is a swipe to the left).

It's interesting to see how guys try to sell themselves. I think a gym photo is always a good thing *if* you go to the gym. If you don't then maybe… just don't post one. I saw a guy testing the power of a horse's back one day. The horse looked like it wanted to commit suicide and I wanted to report him for animal cruelty. I digress. There are a couple of problems with Tinder for me:

1. I don't have a Facebook photo of me, so guys assume I'm trying to catfish or am uber ugly. I tell them I'm a strong 6.5 and can be a 7 if I'm suitably motivated.
2. I hate Tinder

All that aside, I decided that #40DayDating needed Tinder. It's the biggest database of men in London. I couldn't limit myself to websites like OkCupid and PoF because, duh, that would be limiting myself. As for eHarmony, I love you, but you need to do a real Black man recruitment drive. Otherwise I end up with Asians in far flung parts of the country who are just as disappointed as I am when the photo is revealed. Nah. Match and I broke up after a guy tried to recruit me into being a sex worker. I wasn't going back.

Back to Tinder and the no photo thing was proving to be a bugbear. A couple of the guys shouted at me for not having one. I thought to myself, *Then why did you match me if you are so disgusted at my lack of a photo?* I swear some men were on there to troll and vent. I was happy to send one once I knew you weren't operating at a junior school or text-speak level of English. Oh and, I have visual standards too.

10 Dating App Clues That We Aren't a Match

1. You're holding a sedated lion, tiger or snake. This doesn't make you seem brave fam. Set them free!
2. Photos with children that you didn't birth. Why are they online with you when your wife isn't anywhere to be seen?
3. Photos with you standing next to a car. Is it yours or are you still #TeamOysterCard like me? Am I meant to be impressed? I have no clues about cars by the way. I only see colour.
4. Only white friends and/or women. Like dude, you don't have cousins and shit? That one work colleague even if you both aren't in the same team?
5. A photo of a lonesome bottle of Laurent Perrier. Yes, it's pink and may appeal to the ladies but why is this your calling card? Do you want to get me drunk or am I supposed to think you have money? Either way, no thanks.

6. All serious-faced photos with not one smile. I'll assume gold front teeth or missing teeth.
7. Just head shots. I have female friends who are selfie goddesses. I know what this means. Accept your buddha belly like we have to accept ours.
8. You on a camel or with your finger on top of a famous something like the Eiffel Tower, a pyramid, the Taj Mahal, holding up the Pisa Tower… sigh. Just don't be a cliché.
9. A chest shot with you crouched over to make it look like you and the gym didn't break up 12 years ago (that's when we split up too. Ooooh look! We could have had something in common but you're fronting like you still go).
10. Click bait memes about 'what a good woman wants from a real man' followed by an image of a titty or booty. Errr… yeah… no.

Tinder Trials

A Tinder Tease unmatched me 'cos I pointed out that his game was weak, boring and that he whiffed of married. Oh well. The male ego is so fucking fragile! #40DayDating #IAMTrying

When I did start talking to guys I struggled. I didn't know the lingo and pace. At one time I had 13 matches and they were shooting questions at me like this was *Mastermind*. I met a guy who was clearly working for MI5. He wanted to know if I had kids, why I didn't have kids, was I planning to have kids and how many. Didn't mention his kid situation so I was guessing child support was a concern. What was all that about with the interview? He wanted to know if that was my real age. He wanted to know what my real name was. He then asked me for photos. One wasn't enough. He needed more. Then after a few, he concluded that I had nice legs and disappeared. Perhaps he was a boob man?

Then there was the student. How are you a student and telling me it's because you're still finding yourself? How were you still so lost in your 40s? I think he was looking for a bursar. I didn't and still don't have the funds to support him and my travel/concert/clothes habit. Something had to give and it wasn't going to be me.

I met another who couldn't speak in sentences longer than five words. It was to the point yes but bordered on rudeness. "What's your star sign? Where you live? You got a man? You into guys with big..." Let's just say this wasn't looking like my lucky Mr Future Hubby.

I did meet a nice one. I was hopeful and willing to look past the fact that he had the same name as my ex. He mentioned meeting up. Of course, he didn't have my photos yet... let's hope he wasn't a boob guy too. Anyway, more on him later.

Overall though my venture into #40DayDating wasn't going too badly. I decided to keep records, set up a new Facebook profile and add some pictures a few days later. I didn't want to limit my options or get shouted at all the time. And so it started.

Close Shaves or Almost Dates

We need to talk about the ones I released back into the wild without ever meeting.

Tinder had a lot of guys who matched and with whom I spoke to for a while but couldn't ever see myself actually meeting. The investment counts though as these near misses were either not engaged enough, married or way too focused on the physical to risk meeting up with. It sounds weird but you really need to trust your seventh (spiritual and physical safety) sense when it comes to dating on the internet and apps.

I don't mean avoid the ones who are only there for sex as, that would be 95% of them and, it could be what you want. No, I mean those who make you itch or feel uncomfortable just through their actions or words. There's a skill to being that creepy, that fast. I found that as I got into filthy apps the creeps showed themselves early. Look for the signs.

When Godfrey Thinks He's Actually a God

One of my early conversations made me realise how quickly things could escalate on these apps.

God: I know you are going to love me. Everyone loves me. Is Chelsea your real name?

Me: We'll see God. No, that's not my real name.

God: I thought as much… so you think it's time we should know your real name?

Me: Who is we? If we meet, then I will tell you but until then there is really no need.

God: You need to understand how trust works. You clearly don't get it. Trust means we tell each other things and then we can grow to love. Isn't that what you want after all?

Me: Trust! Aah! Thanks for mansplaining that so clearly

God: ha-ha, mansplaining. So you are implying I am patronising. Bitch. What I'm trying to explain to you is that … *blah, blah, blah,* but you don't understand me. The thing is … *blah, blah, blah*

This user has been blocked

PART 2

Let the Dating Be Had

Date 1: Neighbours… Everybody Needs Good…

So after swiping and giggling incessantly with my bestie, I finally started talking to one guy more than the others. Wait, before I continue, I need to make a public service announcement.

Some dudes really need to think about their first and sometimes only photo. Believe me when I say, I've never laughed so hard in my life when I was swiping. Why look at the camera like you're hungry and I'm your next meal? Why pose with a pained expression like you just farted and even you can't take the stench? Yes, we aren't all models but for the love of selfies, learn to take a half-decent picture. As men love to tell women, 'Smile!' You really only have a second to make a swipe impression.

Back to Date 1. He was in his late 40s, 5'8" and worked in some sort of IT field. I never really listen when people tell me what they do. I'm just glad they've got somewhere to be and working during the day. Besides, he didn't live too far away. I'm going to say a mile away although he was rather shady about it when probed (not anally. Not that kind of book!) It turned out he'd moved back in with his family whilst the divorce was going through. This one was worried about me stalking him. I mean, did he honestly think I was going to hang around his mum's house waiting for him to come out? I'm not only lazy but not a fan of the cold.

We exchanged numbers after he sent me 15 different photos of himself and he called me immediately. At first, I thought this was a good thing because, errr, I like a chatty man, but he was not in the best place and I really didn't need to know all about it. I love a good communicator but, upon reflection, this felt like therapy – something I was soon to realise was a common theme from the dating app guys. They needed to talk. A lot. And I didn't.

It was everything from his reasons for having to move back home to his soon to be ex-wife and kids living in the country (to me this means the other side of the M25 and turns out that I was right) to generally describing why life just wasn't where he wanted it to be right now. I get it. Life was a bit shit but does one have to lead with this when dating? I wondered if I too need to come up with some reality TV style hardship to tell on first dates. Can't we just talk about travel and hobbies and Brexit like normal people or is this now a modern way of showing vulnerability? God, I hope not. I'll have to make something up pretty quickly and memorise it.

With all of his personal baggage, I got why he wasn't so trusting at this stage and immediately went into fixer mode. We talked about custody issues, forgiveness, exes and so on and so forth. Surprisingly, I realised that despite not having children of my own, my love of bad American romances and dating way too many dads had given me more understanding of the British legal system than he had. That and I don't think he was willing to fork out for a decent lawyer; more on that later. It's a blessing and a curse to retain such useful information and I actually sounded like an expert. I even found myself thinking that this might be a titbit to add to my dating profiles. Self-taught lawyer.

But in the back of my head was the realisation that I don't like men who so readily slag off their exes on dates. Yes, some relationships are a train wreck, but I don't know this woman and you making her seem like a class-A bitch isn't helping either of us. It also tells me that you have dubious taste in women, if she's all of what you claim. I also know that if we were to date and it was to go wrong, I would be the one you would be cussing out on the first phone call to some other woman. How is that even an acceptable thing? The red flags were out.

We agreed that as we lived so close to each other, we could go running together. I immediately went online and ordered a whole bunch of new exercise clothes. I still couldn't find the missing trainers, so this was more necessity than vanity. No need for him to know that I had accidentally lost a lot of weight recently and didn't actually exercise much (that pesky chronic illness made exercise harder so for once this wasn't me being lazy).

It was all going well until he admitted not wanting any more children. I immediately lost interest as his teenage children didn't sound peachy but agreed to meet as he was local and, maybe I could set him up with someone else. I sent his photos to another single friend who looked him over and determined he wasn't her type. Such a shame as he needed support during this time. She said she needed height.

We met for coffee and he continued with his tales of woe. I would like to say that there was a spark there were it not for the fact that he was, first of all, late. Who bloody doesn't know where VQ is on Fulham Road when they're local? Who walks slowly when they're late and you're waiting outside in the cold trying not to shiver? Then, he was cheap.

"I only had a coffee Chelsea. So, do you need me to contribute?"

It was definitely going to be a no from both of us. How can you not afford the £3 coffee you drank? Were times that hard? I mean, to me if you can't leave your house with at least a tenner for a drink, then you should stay indoors. On top of that, I had my suspicions that his 5'8" claim was a rather generous estimation. Either that or he was slouching from carrying the world on his shoulders. To round off this disaster nicely, he looked like he'd seen 50 and 50 had told him to lie about his age. The man looked weathered.

And we never did go running. Turned out he got really busy on the weekends. We spoke a few times over the course of my dating challenge but mainly about him so, that's really not a strong basis for a relationship. In all honesty, I think I learned that when someone is in the midst of a divorce it's best to leave them the fuck alone. You can't fix everything and especially not a man who is walking shorter than his profile suggests he is.

This date is one reason why you shouldn't remain friends with dates. They start to see you as a resource they can use to talk to about their own dating journey. Months later, he called me after 11pm to tell me he'd met someone. Yay. Coincidentally, I knew the person he was now with and he didn't think we should keep in touch because she might not like it.

I was confused as I think we'd only spoken all of five times since our date… and the last time was six or seven months before he called to share his good news. Why would I give a fuck? I think he thought I gave a fuck which worried me because clearly, I was giving off the 'I give a fuck' vibes. No fucks given. Then, he pissed me off by doing the, 'What about you? Still single?' pity noises bullshit. I listened to 15 minutes of what I might be doing wrong before we signed off.

Fucker. But I'll leave karma to eff this one up. And his ex-wife according to him. Moving on swiftly…

Date 2: The Aggressive One

This one I dismissed before meeting. Straight away I found him aggressive and that's a red flag for me. This type is often a women hater and I can't relax in their company. I'm not stupid enough to believe men who say it's just that one ex who really got under their skin or made them that way. It's just unnecessary to project your hurt feelings or misogyny on new people but they can't seem to help themselves. I also don't take to guys who only use gym photos. It's aggressive and tells me that he's too into the body sculpting thing. I'm not of that world. I'm so allergic to gyms that I don't even try to peek into their darkened windows anymore.

He was pushy in ways that really annoyed me early on by asking me about kids, height, weight, like he was considering purchasing my breeding potential. Yes, we've all watched *12 Years a Slave*.

It was early days and as an early adopter of online dating back in the day, this wasn't an entirely alien experience to me. Some men interview you but are shockingly poor at giving out any information about themselves. Another pet peeve. They assume that they are perfect, and I should be thankful to be in their lives. Typical example – whenever I asked him a question like where in Nigeria he was from, he went quiet. Wait, was I being 419ed? His 'physical' questions annoyed me because how many photos do you think is reasonable to request? This dude was all about the photos. I am not one to share when there are six for you to choose from on my profile. I learned that this is the nude pic dance but again, I now know better. Well, I've learned the hard way!

I was trying not to let my usual irritations get to me. Maybe it was me. This was a 40-day challenge and I was committed to making it work this time. I'm naturally impatient but I had to step out of my comfort zone, right? Maybe I expected too much, like good manners and dating etiquette when in fact they were as bombarded with vagina pics as I was with dick pics? But no, guys just needed to get their shit together.

We agreed to meet up despite the red flags but, the day before we were meant to, he told me to make sure I was wearing a short skirt and heels. I told him where to get off and he seemed rather confused by my attitude. 'What brings this on?' he asked. We argued and I told him he wasn't right. He told me that I took myself too seriously and then started telling me how this was the problem with women. Eventually I blocked him mid-rant.

The block feature is now my best friend. At first, I was shy to use it in case it came back in real life and bit me on the butt. Black London is so very small! But I'm not going to take verbal abuse, aggression and lies from strangers. Life is just too short.

Moving on...

Date 3: The African Debt

With Date 1 under my belt and Date 2 avoided because nobody needs that level of aggression in the flesh, I was feeling more confident. This wasn't so terrible. I could do this! My dating muscles were slowly coming back after a year off training and I got into the groove of swiping on the train to and from work. One hundred swipes each way and 50 at lunch. I had a system!

Then came Date 3. OK, so there were signs, even though he looked cute from the photos but, I'm learning, my singirls. Photoshop is a witchcraft devil tool for those trying to trick you. His didn't look photoshopped. Otherwise surely, he would have photoshopped a tidy house?

We had conversations on WhatsApp during which he told me that he wanted kids straight away as he didn't want to have no retirement babies. I asked him what he meant, and he made some quip about retiring early. He was 41 and already had kids. I just laughed it off as banter. With great pride, he told me that he was Nigerian and that he had been in the UK for about 10 years. I told him that I wasn't averse to him being Nigerian as apparently, he'd been victim to some bad Naija PR. Like I said, there were signs.

Our first date was planned for Westfield White City as it was half an hour door-to-door for me. Most people can get there whether they are driving or being dropped off by their unassuming wives. Some men have no shame.

We arranged to meet at 8pm. He turned up at 8.01 in a smart off-white jacket and smelling of a recent shower. Good. Already I was impressed, and we walked to the food section of the mall. Turns out he'd already eaten so I told him he was welcome to watch me eat to his heart's content. I realised that I was flirting non-sexually. This was a new thing for me, so it kind of took me by surprise so I quickly resorted to quips to hide my discomfort. I thought my flirt had been broken by years of sexual harassment, but it turns out that it was still in there, hiding. That shower scent really worked! I was however not impressed by the 'I've eaten already' move. This happened a lot during my first dating round and I realised that it was code for cheap and only looking for sex.

We went to Bill's restaurant because I knew they would have a gluten-free menu. We did the banter thing, but he was busy with phone calls. I asked him if it was work that kept him on the phone. He had some long-arse job title with technician and other words which was just a fancy way of saying he worked in Local Authority Housing.

Turned out the family in Nigeria couldn't operate without finding out what he was doing every five minutes. Strange that the family were so intense I thought to myself, but who was I to question other people's family set up. Eventually he got off the phone and regaled me with stories of his bad dates. I mention two light ones to keep up but he's on a roll and doesn't require or want any input from me at all.

He needlessly told all of his bad dates about themselves and never paid more than his share of the bill. I got the hint. I dipped another slice of gluten free bread into my chicken liver parfait and ordered two more slices. He was in his zone now. All the dates lied about their looks. All of them. This was the recurring theme. Then, he said he was feeling warm and took his jacket off. Eh eh! Was someone expecting? Whatever jacket that was needed to be patented and sold to uncles all over the world. This man had a buddha belly to rival my own sweet buddha belly, Maxine Saj (yes, my belly had a name and a personality all of her own; see gluten free menu). I shrugged it off because maybe I could suggest a gluten-free life for both of us after a few dates? You see, still, I remained optimistic. All of us have been burned on this dating circuit. And whatever shower gel he used was spellbinding. I really love *'eau de* recent shower' apparently. Maybe it should be made into a car fragrance.

I asked him about his ex as he'd mentioned her and there was a shoulder and facial switch. The dude was still angry because, apparently, she had held him back in life. The vehemence was disproportionate to the 'crime' I thought but, who knows what shit they put each other through? After Date 1, I wasn't going to ask for too many details. I'm nowt if not a quick learner.

He then told me that he was looking to buy a property but could only afford something in some parts of Essex I'd never heard of. Apparently though he could sell his properties in Nigeria that would mean raising just £45K and he couldn't get a single mortgage for anything in London for that. I nodded in sympathy because he wasn't lying although he seemed to be angry at me over this, like I was the one blocking his home ownership dreams. Then he went back to the ex and seemed harrowed as he continued talking about her. I mean I still wasn't clear on how exactly she had held him back except that she had bad credit and no job.

Then I got angry. Angry at the Conservatives because, now people can't afford property in London and I don't want to have to commute 'long-long' to date.

That's not a life. He started asking me about my debt and how I managed it. I told him that I was debt-free but for mortgages. That's when his eyes sparkled and he leaned in to tell me about an offer he was sure I couldn't refuse.

I told him that I wasn't looking to invest in property in Nigeria thanks. He said, "nah this was better than that," and apparently, we would both be winners. He was looking for a woman to take him to the next level and was willing to give me children in exchange for security. Whilst this deal might have sounded great to most, I just didn't see it working for me. It was just all too transactional. He said that he needed £50K and I would get two kids. I mean, why would I pay £50,000 for two children? Was this even a legal suggestion as I'm pretty sure you can't put a price on children or sperm in the UK. Nah, something was starting to smell off.

As he was huffy with me, he didn't contribute to the bill and kept trying to sell me on his plan. In the end, I just gave him some property advice and let him walk me to the tube station. We did the awkward hug goodbye at which point I felt the belly poke me.

It's sad that guys have had to resort to pimping out their sperm all because the London housing market is a hot and twisted mess. I wished him luck on his financial journey and didn't have the heart to break it to him that he was overvaluing his sperm at £25K a child. I still do think he could make a killing from that jacket patent and shower gel though?

—♥—

Date 4: The Golden Nugget

Date 4 was a quick PoF (Plenty of Fish) turnaround from matching to first conversation to meet up. This guy was a find and I wasn't going to linger. He wasn't from London and when we met online, his photo was taken from the side so all I saw was a gorgeous smile. We started talking and his accent was a heavy Caribbean one with a slight inflection of someone who had lived in the North of England at some point. Rather delicious.

He was one of those successfully self-employed tradesmen who wanted to grow his business. I think gas man, but it could have been electrician or plumber or... I kid you not when I say I don't really listen to people's jobs. I did find him communicative and interesting but then this also meant that he felt that he needed to share his feelings about himself. This however didn't come until after the date. Let me backtrack a bit.

He lived in South London and I was in Chelsea, so we agreed to meet at the White Lion in Streatham one night. I think our meeting time was 10pm which was usually the time I headed back from dates, but he said he needed to finish something off. It was closer to midnight when he finally turned up. By that time, I'd been there for 20 minutes as he kept delaying our meeting time. Strike one! I love to be in bed by midnight with my laptop and a nice cup of Rooibos tea! But I was willing to sacrifice my tea for one night. Who knew if he was the one?

When he arrived, he was lovely and tall. I noticed a gold tooth at the front of his mouth. Sigh. I know it was fashionable back in the last century but Goldie he was not. We had a great conversation, very few silences and the sexual attraction was definitely there. I could see myself climbing him. He reminded me of my recent crush and...

I finally called time on proceedings after two cranberry juices for me and two double rums and coke for him. I assumed he had also taken an Uber but turned out he was driving. I didn't really think that in this day and age, anyone needed to drink and drive and he pursed his lips when I made it clear that I wouldn't be getting a lift from him. I mean, I'm just too precious! Strike 2. Drink driving. Urgh. So 1990s!

He also told me that he *loved* Granaries. For those of you not familiar with this horrendous, long-running South London club it's... well horrendous and long-running. Well, no. It's really of a certain era and I was too young to appreciate its charms. My friend's Dad used to go there. Golden Nugget seemed to spend an inordinate amount of time there, alone and drinking, and didn't see that as a problem. Then, he half-invited me to come along giving me the impression that he wasn't that bothered with my company as it was clear that he went there for the booze and the women. I politely declined as I didn't think my spirit could take another minute of him on the spirits. Dude could drink!

After the date, we Whatsapped and spoke a few times. He made it clear that he wanted loads more children and that he wanted them with the same woman.

I had seen him looking down at my hips a few times. I guess I passed the sight hips test. Men.

During one conversation, I explained to him that I was not planning on dating exclusively until I was sure. He told me that I had too much choice and that was a dangerous thing to have apparently. Errr, thanks Golden Dating Guru. He then asked me what I had done that day and I told him I'd just come back from my French class. He had a go at me for wasting my time learning another language and said that I had much better things I could spend my money on. I think he meant him. That didn't go down too well. I was starting to feel that he could be one of those guys who wanted you to live by his rules and his alone. I pulled back mentally because I hate being controlled.

But then, just like that, we both stopped conversing. I suspect he was tired of putting all of this energy into the 'relationship' and my admission that I was dating others didn't sit well with him. I didn't like the fact that he was such a heavy drinker-driver. Choose your vice but don't put others at risk.

It's a bit of a shame as maybe with time we could have worked something out, but we were at that age where nobody wants to change. I guess the flame went out of the gasman.

Date 5: The Sinful Catholic

This may have been my fault. I admit to finding those who led with their religion slightly uptight. We had been talking for a few days and I just wanted to move things on a bit you know? I was also in a bit of a flippant mood which made tease anyone who don't have a sense of humour. But then in my defence doesn't he deserve it for not having a sense of humour? You decide:

Dude: I'm Catholic. It's an important part of my life

Me: Good for you. I'm not religious at all

Dude: I think everyone is entitled to their views and I don't know the Bible well enough to debate it

Me: Good, good

Dude : But I do think… *20 minutes later…* and that's why my God is the only Lord and Saviour and the best.

Me: silence

Dude: Chelsea? Hellooo!

Me: I fell asleep

Dude : Really?

Me: No

Dude: You crack me up. You're so funny!

Me: (stares at the screen blankly thinking of ways to harm him)

Here's another excerpt in case you have yet to decide:

Dude: Both are my official names

Me: Ok a confirmation name is not an official name, but you can call me Bernadette

Dude: By official names I mean names that appear on my official documents.

Dude (again): You look great in your profile picture.

Me: Thanks

Me (again): OK I hate to labour the point, but I don't consider my confirmation certificate an official document. I don't even know where it is. So, are you religious?

Dude: OK but I'm not talking about confirmation certificates, but educational qualifications, passports etc

Dude (again): I'm a sinner and Catholic forever. I wish to sin less

Me: You wish to sin less on Tinder? That's an interesting angle. So what does that mean? Confess your existing sins so that I can understand

Dude: Well, I'm not a murderer or rapist but just like to emphasise that I do not consider myself a holy or righteous man

Me: Ok I just assumed extra-marital sins. Good to know you're not a murderer or rapist

Dude: I'm not married. I'm divorced.

Me: Ok…

Dude: I assume you're single.

Me: No

Me (again): I'm married to Jesus Christ our Lord and Saviour. But only the Black Jesus. Not the white one with the strawberry blondeness.

Dude: OK

Me: How's Tinder going for you?

Dude: Not great on the British side… If I were to move to Hungary or Austria or Germany, I'd not be lacking women… British women seem to be particularly difficult

Dude (again): I'm very straightforward and like to meet up ASAP rather than chat endlessly

Dude (yet again): But I understand that women are oversubscribed here

Me: You have far-reaching tastes I see. Like your hero, Jesus. He travelled far and wide helping all sorts of women.

Me (again): Oversubscribed? I think it's just a numbers game. So, no luck so far, huh?

Dude: What do you mean that Jesus travelled far and wide helping all sorts of women?

Me: Well, wasn't he spreading the word and helping prostitutes and all people find God? Like Mary Magdalene?

Dude: So you don't believe in Our Lord Jesus Christ?

Me: I believe he existed, yes

Dude: You don't believe He is God?

Me: Errr… what's the question?

Side note: I don't think we should talk about religion, sex or politics with just anyone but, definitely not with those that are religious, sexual or political before you meet them. I've learned and bow my head in lapsed Catholic shame at how I behaved. This poor man was just trying to get into my knickers and here's me teasing him about strawberry-blonde Jesus. Anyway, believe it or not, the conversation continued!

Me: Can I just assume we aren't a match?

Dude: I'm open-minded enough to relate to anybody even if we disagree

Me: That's magnanimous of you

Dude: But you indicated that you're married?

Me: No. I was kidding. I don't think we get each other.

Dude: Ok. What are you up for if you don't mind...

Me: Up for?

Dude: I'm sorry if that was the wrong way to put it. What are you looking for... casual relationship or serious? As for me, any!

Me: Oh, serious.

Me (again): You know I don't think you're taking this sinning less thing very seriously if you're up for both or anything. What would Jesus say?

Dude: Please keep the name of God out of it!

Me: Ok dude, calm down. I'm out. Take care.

The funny thing with this one is that he then changed his photos and I didn't realise that it was him, so we spoke again a month or so later before I realised that it was him! I quickly told him that we couldn't chat again as he was way too pious for my heathen ways and he agreed. So it ended well enough eventually. But then years later he reached out again!

Dude: OK, now I remember you! You did fancy me anyway. But you haven't got any pic here.

Me: Are those your kids? *[new information not previously mentioned]*

Dude: Yes

Me: You're predominantly into white women I remember you saying. Why are you reaching out after so long? Are you bored?

Dude: You remembered or you imagined me saying that? You rejected me that's why we didn't meet.

Me: Nope you were all about better chances in Europe *[oh the Brexit irony eh?]*

Me (again): So if I rejected you why are you looking to trouble me now? Do you think my criteria might have changed?

Dude: Do you still have our chat. I had totally forgotten the number.

Me: On Tinder, no, but you were bemoaning your lack of success with the ladies.

Dude: Not sure I remember myself making a big issue about that. I will always say I find British women the most difficult to meet!

Me: Ok so it's still a no from me, Mr. Up-For-Anything-Three-Years-Later. We aren't a match. But you stay blessed yeah.

Dude: OK Miss Still Single and Angry

Me: Why would I be angry with you? I'd forgotten about your very existence. I sent a stay blessed as a nod to your religious beliefs and faith that Jesus will help you find what you seek. Stay blessed dude!

Hmmm, I guess it didn't end as well one had hoped and prayed for. Oops! Nevertheless, I decided to do ten Hail Marys, a shot of Apple Schnapps and some chocolate in penance. Shit, I'm out of Apple Schnapps and Hail Marys. Shit, I can't drink anymore. Shit, chocolate it is!

—♥—

Date 6: Kilburn Half Pint Hotep

Online dating can be depressing. I only seem to meet hoteps, friends or Dwights and things I enjoy like concerts and my friends are now selfish or smug. Any ideas? #40DayDating #TinderFatigue"

So, to cut a long story short, it didn't go well. We hadn't spoken on the phone and so I had nobody to blame but myself. I shouldn't meet people before a telephone interview. I learned that through this date.

This dude – let's call him Kilburn – and I matched on Tinder. He said he was in his 40s. I guess he had been once. Like a decade before. He didn't say much by text, but his photos were cute enough. He did seem to have a strange concept of time and distance. He talked about how Chelsea was only five minutes from Kilburn, and I replied, "How, by flight?" Weird.

Anyhoo, on the last Sunday of the Premiership, I was off to a Samuel Jack gig and asked if he wanted to go. He said yes. I told him 8pm. He must have misread or thought that this was a suggestion as he arrived at 9.25. The event finished at 10.15. Apparently, he was at the Arsenal game so was tired but also still had to go via Cricklewood to drop something off at a friend's house. I was already wary when he said he was an Arsenal fan because they would be unbearable on this day, the day they finished second and ahead of Spurs but, Cricklewood too? And he wasn't driving. Hmmmm... my datey senses were on high alert.

He came in and at first, I didn't see him because Tinder still hadn't responded to my yet-to-be-written emails about adding height to their profiles. Dude was battling to be my height and... I'm short.

I saw him looking around the room and I almost didn't wave him over but I was the only black person, other than a male singer, in the room so he would have seen me anyway. He came over and it soon became apparent that the 43 on his profile was a dream deferred. I have no problem with older but, don't lie and think you will get away with it. This dude had lived a hard life, died and lived two more. He was old. And he was JBJ – Jamaican Born Jamaican – and I was just getting way too many, 'I watched *Yardie* on repeat' vibes from him.

Without apology he asked me why I'd taken an Uber earlier and I said, because it's cheap and I like to be on time. This was not the right answer. According to him, I was not meant to take cabs because they're too expensive. He'd only taken a black cab twice in his whole life! I don't know how one lives in London and doesn't drive or take black cabs but, ok... I guess we were all different. For one I'm normally on time. Yes, I was still smarting. The cost of Ubers was to be a recurring theme.

He then told me that he only listened to early rap and lovers' rock. Apparently, music had to be the type that you could grab your partner and grind to. I assumed this was the lovers' rock not the rap. I smiled to myself as we were at an acoustic unsigned artists thing in an industrial unit in Willesden. Whenever the artists asked us to get involved and clap or sing, he sat there (on the floor) all stoosh, looking like he wanted to fight them. They were young people. They were trying. I had to flap my hands around doubly hard to compensate for Half Pint. He also didn't like the sitting on the floor thing. Clearly this was not one to take to festivals.

We talked about gigs and he said that I couldn't go to gigs if I had kids. I told him the dad can stay at home with the kids and he looked at me like I stole his last angry argument. This dude was just too hard and, well, angry. Perhaps he was having a bad day but I suspect this was just him. Wait, Arsenal lost! Duh.

When the event was done and as we were making our way out, he tried to suggest hanging out but, what for? Then the real bullshit started as the lecturing kicked off. Apparently, all successful black men go for white women because... Jews... wait, what? I didn't get the connection and so he mansplained. It was some antisemitic conspiracy theory which, when questioned, fell apart. Then he proceeded to lecture me on Africa and why South Africans needed to reclaim their land and how he had spent two weeks in West Africa (The Gambia then) and how as a people we needed to rise. This from a guy who had a whole heap of photos featuring video vixens on his phone! How did I know this? When he'd shown me photos of his grown kids, he was thwarted by a deluge of porn babe pictures. Oops!

Then it hit me! I was on a date with a Hotep. This could never, ever work. I'm so not the one because I don't want to be told how to be a black queen/empress/sister/woman. I'm happy listening to my pop and rock and soul and wearing my hair how I like it and I don't do the Egyptology thing because it's not the only culture of Africa. I'm comfortable in my black identity without having to appropriate a generic 'AfriKan' one for those in the diaspora. I felt duped though because he wasn't in a *dashiki*, nor was his hair in dreadlocks, so I didn't recognise him 'out of uniform'. How was I to know that he was a swirl of conspiracy theories and misogyny wrapped in royal salutations like empress and ’my queen’?

We made it to the overground only to find out that it would be 21 minutes until the next train. Fuck it. I got my phone out and booked an Uber. He tried to argue with me that it was a waste of money and unsafe but by then my stubborn Taurus side had come out and I wasn’t having it. Besides, the Uber driver looked like a sweetheart. When I got home, he sent me one last message. Nah fam, I’m not the one.

This dating thing was becoming frustrating. Six dates and four of them were knobheads. Really? That’s a 67% knob factor. I went home feeling deflated and tired when I realised that I was still attracting duds. It was time to do something different like… speak to them on the phone first.

Then I remembered that there was dairy-free custard and bananas at home. Nothing is ever that bad, right? I just wish these dudes were more transparent on their profiles. Be clear! Say, “I’m a Half Pint Hotep” and leave us ’non-hoteps’ alone.

Please Don't Just Say Hi!

M*e on my Tinder profile*: Oh, and please don't just say *hi*. I won't respond.

Guy 1: Hi

Guy 2: Hiya

Guy 3: Hey Gorgeous/Beautiful/Sexy

Guy 4: *[cut and paste]* Hello my wonderful Princess. My name is Prince. I love you. 'You're' smile, your beautiful eyes. 'Your' the flower that is missing from my garden. When can I meet you? Where do you 'leave'? I can't wait to get to meet you and show you the love that is in my heart. My number is XXXXXXXXXXXX and I can't wait to hear 'ur' sweet, loving voice. Hurry. We are not getting any younger *[end cut and paste]*

Deletes all

Let's start this again shall we? #40DayDating #NonsenseGoats

It was at this point that I realised that I seriously needed a Tinder break…

PART 3

Dating Dads

Date 7: Cute Daddy Dude – My Three-Day Blunder

Phrases I've Come to Loathe From Wastemen:

"I must give you some money for that."
Here's me thinking, we're both looking at the bill. So is his pocket too far for him to reach? #40DayDating #StayHome

Tinder was on pause and I reluctantly went back to PoF so I wasn't expecting much. Turns out PoF was winning though.

Before meeting, we spoke on the phone (I'm learning!) and it was clear that though quite expressive he was also just a tad bit ditzy. It took him a while to realise that Chelsea wasn't an African family name and that maybe if he wanted to buy and sell stuff like cars, he would need space to store them somewhere other than on the street. He'd gotten in trouble with the council already. This is exactly why I don't ask people about their jobs. He wanted to flip cars he said. But he was keeping them outside his house and the council weren't having any of it. I thought, *Good. Why must the neighbours lose valuable parking spaces?* However, he was a dad of two kids whom he seemed to adore, was ambitious and did I mention, he was cute? Photos are the devil. And I was a sucker for a cute face apparently even if he wasn't saying much else.

I asked him if he had the kids on the weekend and he seemed surprised that I knew that it was his weekend. I explained that it was a 50/50 chance with these things though I think he didn't believe that I wasn't stalking him. Err, yeah. This is him. I know, my singirls; I can't say that the signs weren't there. Anyway, we decided to meet on a Monday.

Monday

He was half an hour late and blamed it on parking. This was in Clapham Junction where there's a whole big Asda parking. He met me at Revolution and then decided that he couldn't eat anything on the menu which he barely glanced at because, get this, it was English food. I asked him how long he'd been here from Nigeria and he said, "Since I was two." So a whole 35 years and including school dinners, that didn't teach your palette how to eat English food? No, he wanted to go to Nando's. I told him that I'd had Nando's for lunch and I wasn't feeling it twice in one day. He insisted and I acquiesced because with his lateness I was actually quite hungry. Besides, Nando's is my national dish anyway.

We got there and ate. The whole night we were catching joke and teased each other. I was on full snark that night and my flirt was truly back! Despite that, he didn't even want to pay for the whole meal. Then he was pretend mad because

I didn't bother to get him a drink which wasn't very wifey of me. In the end, he put in a whole £20, even after arguing that I should pay. Yay.

There was a bit of kissing in the car, but it wasn't to my taste. Way too much heavy tongue and poking. He dropped me off onto my street then was annoyed when I hadn't sent a text three hours later. This joker. How was I to know that he wasn't pretending. Therein lies the flaw in WhatsApp. Note to self – ask for voice messages.

Tuesday

The next day he sent a text because he had decided that he wanted to be real with me and didn't want me dating anyone else. I didn't understand but I said that I would consider it… which I did for 15 whole minutes before deciding that I actually did enjoy dating and that I was going to continue doing so. Besides – that awful kiss! I broke the news to him as I was walking home through Battersea Park and had to endure 12 minutes of break up. Yes, breakup. This dude was going on like we were something already. We had met the night before.

Apparently, I was meant to have been so blown away by the kiss that I should have been hooked. Unfortunately for me, I don't appreciate having a tongue stuffed into my mouth, searching for my tonsils. I have a small mouth. So yeah, the kiss was not the thing that was going to swing it for him. But he thought it would. My thing is this: I don't like to waste anyone's time and now that I'd seen that possessive and immature trait in him, I wasn't going to let the memory of a few good jokes deter me. It wasn't really worth the aggro. So, I stuck to my guns and eventually convinced him that it wasn't going to happen.

There I was sighing about it on social media as you do and turns out that someone else had dated him and received exactly the same texts! So this is a thing? Dude likes to play intense and mess with women's emotions? Thank God for that kiss. My heart will go on.

Wednesday

The next day he'd had a change of heart or spoken to his friend. Who knows? He wanted to be friends. I said no problem. He asked if we could still go out that Friday but I'd already made other plans. Then it escalated quickly. I had sensed the underlying aggression from the texts but was willing to try the 'friends thing'. What I hadn't anticipated was him going off on a whole nation. Sorry South Africa. He accused me of being fast and easy because apparently all women were like that in South Africa and that was why the HIV rate was so high there and that I wasn't attractive anyway, but he had been willing to look past that because *blah, blah, blah.*

And herein lies the problem with internet dating. Some people think you are in a relationship less than 24 hours after you meet and after one conversation. Some think they can control how you date. And then some are just plain, wasteman crazy and all you need to do is 'run, my singirls, run. Grab that cute purse and run like the wind!

Scores on the doors so far? Two PoF and five Tinder. I've liked 50% of the PoF and 20% of the Tinder dates so, I'm guessing PoF is a better bet. That said, the numbers are so different in terms of exposure to men that I shouldn't be so hard on poor Tinder. They don't have a wasteman detector.

My verdict on Cute Dad? Nutter. Bad kissing and a boob squeeze do not a relationship make. Oh yeah, I hadn't mentioned the boob squeeze. Nowt to write home about there either. It was like a tyre pressure poke more than a squeeze. Urgh!

This wasn't going well. Next!

Wait… four months later and Cute Dad Dude tried to apologise for his behaviour.

Cute Dad Dude: Hope you're well. I sincerely regret my behaviour last time and I was bang out of order. There's no excuse for the way I spoke to you and you didn't deserve it. I'm honestly sorry and I hope we can move on and maybe start again as friends.

P.S. How's the dating scene coming along? I see you're still fishing lol…)

I didn't even have the energy to respond to him and blast him. And he reminded me that I'd forgotten to deactivate my PoF account. Fuckeries. I guess that the dating wasn't going well for him either, huh?

—♥—

Almost Dates: Black Santa

This is a short but bitter one. He claimed to be 38 which is the new sweet age lie for men who like or think they should be entitled to date younger women. He worked for the NHS which tells me nothing, had one child and a gorgeous smile. I claimed to believe him on everything until we transferred the conversation to WhatsApp when I realised that he was a delusional liar.

For those who are unclear, a lie must always be within the realms of believability, right? Who was this grandad staring back at me?!? He looked like Will Smith in Hancock but 30 years older after the alcohol had changed him forever. Like he'd been drinking for days and not bothered to shave or give a shit about life. Why was he leading with this photo when the ones on Tinder were cute and fresh?

I took a second look at the batch on Tinder and they were clearly dated. That '90s hip-hop pose and hairstyle said it all. Then the wallpaper and interiors, now that I had turned Inspector Suspicious, were a dead giveaway (unless it was his mum's or gran's house in which case it's looked the same since 1965).

I asked him how old his photos were and at first he thought it was a joke question. He started laughing but when I didn't back down, he started abusing me, calling me rude and insensitive and all that. OK, maybe saying that he looked like Black Santa was not so polite but, in my head, with those wrinkles, beard and weight he *did* look like Black Santa... the one that lives in my head anyway. I mean this dude must have been the same age as Bruce Forsythe's older brother or was in the same class as Winston Churchill. This was not good. He was a Class A liar.

And therein lies the problem with liars. They are indignant when ousted. Nobody likes to be caught out in a lie. On top of that, he wasn't a very nice person and his attacks highlighted how much he didn't like women. I'm glad I found out sooner rather than later but this one left a bitter taste in my mouth.

A few weeks later, I started a second Tinder account when I decided that my anonymous one was bringing all the curious and weird to the yard but not a lot of milkshake (I actually don't know where I was going with that analogy. I'll need to listen to that song again). My admin was out of control. This profile had my face on it, and we matched *again*. It took me a while to realise that it was him because he looked *so* much younger 20 years ago, that it threw me again for a second. Obviously, I liked the look of him back in the '90s but that beard that had given up on life and lack of moisturiser will haunt me for a long time. It can't be Christmas every day of the week, right?

Date 8: Army Baby Daddy

My first week with my second Tinder account and I was matched with an army guy. Weird, as I'm not a typical woman who has a men-in-uniform thing so, despite my better judgment, I decided on a swipe right. His messages were polite though not very detailed at all but eventually he asked if he could take me out on a date. I said cool and we agreed on a Tuesday. Then he called me to change the time and I realised he was JBJ. I wasn't expecting that but, OK; besides I loved an accent. We agreed to meet at 9pm. I swear these dates were getting later and later. Did they not realise I needed my sleep?

The morning of our date he decided to send me some flowery morning message on WhatsApp. I'm not a morning person and I hate cut and paste messages so I tried to crack a joke which he didn't get. I realised that I was going to have to keep my snarky levels to a minimum and my quips totally in check. This was like telling someone with Tourette's Syndrome to hold it in. It just makes it worse. I was trying!

He called me again to say that we could meet at 8.30. Fine. I left my flat at 8.10 and, at 8.20, he tried to text me with some nonsense. I asked him what his ETA was going to be, and he didn't even know what ETA stood for. I thought this was a bit weird for an army person.

I was confused. He was the one that wanted it to be earlier. I mild-ranted on Facebook then I figured, as we were meeting at Westfield's, let me get my shop on.

Dear Westfield,

Why is your HMV so small with hardly any music?

Yours sincerely,

Me

That didn't help my mood. Fifty-seven minutes later, the dude turned up and I had to go and meet him at the station because he didn't know London and definitely not a posh place like Shepherd's Bush? Err, OK.

I asked him how it was that he was in the army and he didn't know what ETA was? What army was this? *Dad's Army*? He looked at me all confused and I realised that, straight away, I'd been snarky. Oh well, you can't keep a good snarky lass down. And as he hadn't grown up in the UK, *Dad's Army* went over his head. We did the awkward hug and with no apology headed to Bill's. On the way, he told me he couldn't drive as his license was taken away after drink-driving. I was nearly ready to say, 'Let's cancel this right now'. How is that your opening gambit?

We get to Bill's and he orders a Heineken and starts telling me about himself. This went on for at least an hour. How he was one of 20-odd children and the youngest and how he had so many kids by three different women and two were the same age, three months apart. On top of that, he wanted more kids but with the same woman who will then look after his kids as their own when he was on tour of duty because apparently the mothers are OK with that.

Then he shared with me how his ex-girl cheated on him and how he thought that all women were bitches and witches and how he's now realised that maybe some aren't, but the majority are. Then it was how he was getting the recruits to dismantle a gun and put it back together. Why I don't know because I had shown no interest in army stuff at all. Then he moved on to Afghanistan and Germany where this man had given him something which gave him diarrhoea for two whole days. Suddenly, my chicken liver parfait didn't seem so appetising. To summarise it all, he closed with how he wanted to leave the army at some point but didn't have a plan, wanted to be a sergeant but didn't have a plan, wanted to have more kids but, yes, you guessed it, didn't have a plan.

Dear God. This was all too much to take in. I told him he should write a book and he looked a bit confused like his life was normal. I was exhausted by the end of his monologues and this is me, who doesn't tire easily. He then looked at me and asked if I had any children. I said no and he said, "Ah, mi see you not ready for kids and all that, innit? Still too selfish." I told him I was ready for kids but not the 'all that'. I mean step-mummy I could be, but this just sounded like a full-time job with no benefits. And how did he get to call me selfish when I'd not even had a chance to tell him anything about myself?

The bill came and he watched me pay. I thought he'd said he was taking me on a date, but I don't think the grand total of £19.41 was in his plans. Not that he even looked at the bill. I didn't even get a thank you for the Heinekens. Needless to say, I was ready to bust out of there and get home to my bananas and custard… again.

We walked back to the train and he told me he would escort me all the way to my door. I guess he'd figured I was fuckable by then. I told him it was a bit too late to try the gentleman moves. He looked confused and asked me how far Chelsea was from here. I told him straight, "You were late, it's late and by the time we both get back the trains won't be running so you will have to take a cab." He said he didn't mind taking a cab and gave me a lascivious up and down look. Nah fam, I'm not the one. And wait, you didn't pay for dinner but now you've got your *likkle* cab money? I'm the one who should have taken a cab earlier.

I had to tell him no again as we got to the station. Then the dude gave me a look that said he was going to stand his ground and argue with me. I mean, really? This date was a mess! Luckily the dating goddesses looked down on me as we were standing there; just then, I spotted someone I barely knew and engaged her in conversation until the train came. As soon as the doors opened, I said a rushed goodbye to my acquaintance and Army Baby Daddy, then I jumped into the train. On the way home, he sent vague WhatsApp messages that I responded to mono-syllabically. I started to wonder if it was too much to expect a normal date with a normal person. Someone who could turn up on time with no madness and no plans to tie you to his kids. Really... was it too much to ask... really?

Anyway, the next day was Hot Gym Dude day. I was starting to think that it would be just fine if he didn't speak. I'd given him allowances already based on *that* body! But, more on him later!

—♥—

Date 9: Hot Gym Dude

Another Tinder date and this one was short on words which I didn't mind as the match alert had pinged on my way home from the misery that was Date 3 (The African Debt).

I remembered this one because all of his photos were in the gym hence his name, Hot Gym Dude. His leading photo didn't show his face, just his biceps and pecs which filled the photo with tattoos and oil, making them look even more defined and… OK, my singirls, this was a completely physical choice. He hadn't written anything witty on his profile which is normally what reeled me in. He kept pushing me for my photos and I thought, *he's not going to want to keep chatting when he finds out that I'm so not Hot Gym Chick.* How was I going to break it to him that I was allergic to gyms?

We swapped numbers quickly (he really was not much of a conversationalist and, as soon as he got my number, he WhatsApped and just said, "You cute, ah wan you. Thank God am single."

Next thing, he called me. I looked at the screen for a second, perplexed, as guys tend to not call just in case the Mrs hears them from the other room. I picked up the phone and said hello like I wasn't sure who it was. I wasn't.

OMG! His voice was sexy. From some small Caribbean island with a roughness and deepness that Morgan Freeman would envy. I was hooked. I really was becoming such a sucker for an accent. And then it hit me! This could be my *How Stella Got Her Groove Back* date. Everyone needs one and let's face it, we weren't really going to do any talking.

He lived in Surrey, which was near my current workplace, so it made sense we were matched. There were children but he claimed he wasn't with the mother. Who knows anymore? He sent me pictures of the kids and I cooed appropriately whilst I plotted ways to get into their daddy's tight jeans. He'd been in the army which freaked me out as I'd never met anyone in the army and now, with Army Baby Daddy, this made two in one week. I was no good at following orders. Anyway, he was now a civilian. He'd been in the army to get citizenship basically. This was something he told me lots of Caribbean people did which was news to me.

There was a slight moment of doubt when he proudly announced that he was a selfie king on Instagram and then proceeded to send me the same day pose of him in the car. Something told me that if we were to have sex it would involve mirrors. Lots of mirrors. I looked at my buddha belly as he asked when we should go on the date and I said, "Let's leave it until next week." If I did seven days of the plank challenge and wore new M&S control tights, I could get away with it at least until we got each other's clothes off. Yep, I had plans for this one and he had plans for me. It was just a case of coordinating Dates 3-6 so that I would have plenty of time for him. OMG I couldn't wait for Date 9!

A week later and I was ready. Like, really ready. He called me that morning to confirm plans and he said that he could only meet at 7pm. The reason?

“Mi wan’ go home and tek a shower so mi a go smell *sweet* fa ya.”

I made some weird sound between a whimper and a purr as I sat at my desk at work in a tight red dress and heels. Yes, everyone in the office knew I was going on a ’fuck me’ date. I was stating my intention loud and clear. Universe. You know I need this.

After work, I waddled to the meeting place in Clapham Junction and tried to pose seductively as I waited for him to arrive. Seven turned into 7.15pm and I WhatsApped with that feeling of dread rising up if he didn’t answer straight away.

Two minutes later, the ticks turned blue. Ten minutes later, I sent a scowling emoji because this is England and I dressed to seduce not to stand outside Clapham Junction like I’m trying to pick up local johns. It so happened that a couple of said local johns didn’t get this memo and gave me the once over. I returned the favour with a scowl and returned to my pose – one that strategically hid my buddha belly but only for 16 seconds at a time. It was too cold for this bullshit. I knew I should have planked harder during the week. I look down and he was now 30 minutes late, so I gave him a call.

“Five minutes! Mi five minutes away!” he shouts down the phone at me.

Maxine Saj and I went back to waiting and watching as one bus after another, heading to my home, passed me by. My shoes hurt because I wasn’t used to wearing heels and I’d already broken my ’half-an-hour-date-wait rule’ for the second time that week. The promise of sex made me weak, what could I say. I limped to the bus stop and decided it was time to call it quits. Now 7.49pm I got on the bus and immediately called Date 1 to bitch about Date 9. He knew them all by now. Date 9 then WhatsApped to say that he'd reached… 53 minutes too late!

And so Date 9 never really happened but, as I was at the designated spot and waiting an inordinate amount of time for him to 'reach', I felt it should count. His being late meant that he was either trying to get away from a woman as work was not the factor or, he was with a woman and wasn't in a hurry to get away. Anything else and he would have explained on the phone.

I'm not going to lie my singirls, I've thought about those biceps from time to time but there was really nothing to be done as we were both proud. Anyway, I'd decided that sex during the challenge would have been confusing for all concerned. Or for me – it would have been confusing for me.

Hot Gym Dude did reach out months later but, stubbornly, I refused to answer. Guess he wasn't that single after all, huh?

Date 10: Sad Dad

My dude friend from Zimbabwe is literally just in a relationship. Like the kettle is still warm. Never married. A year older than me. He has the cheek to ask why I'm being so fussy when there are plenty of men out there? I asked where. He's still thinking 24 hours later. #40DayDating #IHaveQuestions

So the next day I was not in the best of moods after having had a no show/late show date with Hot Gym Dude. Yes, I was still sulking! Then out of the blue, I got a message from a guy who asked if he could call me. We'd chatted a few times on Tinder and I knew where he worked (far far) and lived (far). This was on a Thursday morning on my way to work. He worked in care and was just coming off a night shift so was calling me before he went home to bed.

It was a weird conversation as I struggled to hear most of what he was saying. It was partly because he was very softly spoken and partly because of the joyful noise of the train announcer who seemed to be on one that day. I told him that

I was going to have to speak to him later as I was struggling and besides, his story of having his child taken away from him was not helping to lift my mood.

On the Saturday, I had a surprise birthday party to attend in East London. Didn't he say he lived that way too? So I asked him if he wanted to meet up after the party. Plans made, I set about the arduous task of staying in bed and eating chocolates and Jelly Babies all day.

Now, this was not as easy as one would think as there are absolutely never enough Jelly Babies in the house so you would eventually have to get dressed, head out and buy some more. Or ration. I decided to ration. I'm too lazy for getting dressed twice in one day and so I felt really disciplined. I do have will power. Luckily, I also had blank birthday cards in the house so stayed in bed even more happily.

That evening, I got to the party which was a family affair with lots of old faces I hadn't seen since my friend's wedding a few years before. I actually love family parties. Everyone was happy and this one cracked me up what with the church vibe. You've got to love charismatic Christians for their persistence alone as they turned popular songs into Christian ones.

Every song sounded familiar, be it rap, ragga, soca or RnB, but they were sure to mention Jesus and God a lot to make it legit. I coughed back tears of laughter but I did make note of their commitment and effort. This time nobody tried to recruit me to the church so I had an even better evening.

We caught up on children and exes and dates and husbands and work and then I figured that it was time to go and meet my date. He wanted to join me at the party, but I really didn't know what I was working with, so I told him best we not be rash. Besides, it gave me a good excuse to leave before the cake which wasn't gluten free. The struggle is real.

I rushed over to Westfield Stratford and after a lot of confusion about the entrances, he walked over the bridge to come and meet me. This would have been very romantic if he was as tall as he had said he was instead of three inches shorter. Did I mention I was in four-inch heels? Anyways, we walked to the bars and restaurants. He had no idea where to go and we just ended up in Balans. My Royalty card helped, and I knew they wouldn't be staying open all night like the one in Soho. An escape was on the cards.

We sat and he took forever to order. Like seriously, the menu was not that difficult to decipher. Eventually he went for a salad and I opted for the scallops and some fries. Yes, I ate at the party, but I didn't have cake, remember?

I can't honestly say that I had much to contribute as he started telling me about the traumatic end to his relationship which had practically left him homeless and now abandoned. This went on and on. He seriously wasn't over it. I know he had left out a lot about his contribution to the demise but he mentioned a car and being reckless with money. So I couldn't say I could blame her. Bankruptcy wasn't fun with a young kid and a man who wanted a new car.

The service at Balans was not that swift. So I sat and listened and felt all the laughter from the party seep out of me. He was evidently depressed. At one point it had certainly been clinical depression and although he was doing better, he still had a long way to go. I asked about his other dates and he said that they hadn't gone anywhere after the first one and he wasn't sure why. One had even blocked him.

I told him that I didn't think he was ready to date and gently suggested that he sought some counselling. He had done incredibly well to pull himself this far, but everyone could use a little help to get over the last bit of something so traumatic (I hoped that by using his language he would understand me).

Eventually, I think he did and we left. I figured we were on the same page, i.e., we were not even reading the same book of love at all but, the subsequent WhatsApp messages suggested otherwise. I knew I was going to have to have a talk with him as he clearly saw me as a bargain counselling option. Thing is though, I didn't have the energy to date and counsel someone who was so seriously low. Besides, I probably needed a little counselling myself after Tinder. My level of cynicism had increased dramatically.

Here's wishing him the best of luck because there's nothing funny about trauma and depression. Just that finding therapy on Tinder or Bumble may not be your best bet.

PART 4

Dating Duds

Date 11: Catfish Carl

So this one was a Tinder date and after he answered my deal breaker question correctly (Which is the best type of Haribo pack?) we fell into easy conversation. It was a Sunday, I had shopping and cleaning to do so to be honest any distraction was welcome.

Turned out he was coming out of a six-year relationship with an older woman who lived outside of London. He was now renting but I definitely noticed that the transition from 'in something' to 'out of something' was ongoing. He told me about the relationship and where it went wrong and to be honest, I think as her kids grew up, she grew tired of having a 42-year-old child in the house too. But there was something really likeable about him and I'd not laughed like that with a guy in a while. I felt a connection. Date 11 was looking promising indeed.

He was my height which as a tomboy wasn't a problem as I could legitimately wear converse to every single date. We chatted about a lot of things and the banter flowed. He talked about how hard it was out there for a short man and

I made the appropriate cooing noises. "Look, it's hard out there for everyone." I said. This dating lark wasn't a joke. You had to go through all this shit to get the one person you can maybe tolerate for more than a few consecutive dates. It's a part-time job!

We agreed to a meeting on a Tuesday in Hammersmith outside the Millie's Cookies stand. This was just an excuse for me to buy cookies as I'd forgotten about being gluten free but, he wasn't to know this. Then I had the audacity to ask him if his name, Carl, was his real name. He hesitated and said yes. My Spidey senses went into overdrive as I had a feeling of déjà vu. I asked him again and he said all would be revealed when we met.

The next day we were texting and I asked him to send a photo as I need to send it to my DDSS – Designated Dating Security Sister. The DDSS is an important role in a single woman's life as someone must always know where you are and with whom. It's imperative that you give them as much detail as you can. Poor Linda had been overworked of late and was struggling to keep them all straight in her head. Photos were therefore a must.

Then this dude started asking way too many questions like, "Was I a man?" Really? You spoke to me yesterday, saw my photos and now you're doing the gender check? I told him to quit stalling and with that he sent me a photo. Now the photo on Tinder was of a square-jawed someone with brooding eyes and those lips that made you think of mouth-watering Opal Fruits adverts (if you're too young to remember Opal Fruits, you are too young to be reading this). I hadn't found him attractive, but he hadn't offended me in any way.

This was not the same effect that was induced with the photo he sent me which was of someone completely different. This guy was overweight, round-faced with lips that looked like they could swallow you. On top of that, he wasn't even smiling. It was not mouth-watering at all… and, to top it all off, it was taken in a field making him look like he'd just buried a dead body. I asked him if it was his cousin. I was still hopeful you see. We joked around that question a bit. He said that both of them were him but that they were taken 24 years apart. What was this? *Back to the Future* but in different locations with two different people? I called him because it hit me that I had just been catfished, yet he still insisted that he was the same person in both photos.

We argued and he said that he knew I wouldn't want to meet him now because I didn't like what I'd seen. Initially I had agreed to still meet him the next day but a later conversation with a friend made me realise that he was a liar and not to be trusted. If he lied about the simple things like this, then he would be taking another selfie of himself after he'd buried me in the same field. This was not the happily ever after story I was looking for.

He's no longer on Tinder now and said he won't return. I did hear from him a few weeks later when he said that he felt that we'd gotten on really well, so should still meet up. Needless to say, by then I'd moved on because, time waits for no woman and a catfish is just too damn risky for me to contemplate swimming with every day.

Dates 12 & 13: The Tale of Two Dates in Two Cities

Ok so this one was a bit of a mess from the word go and sort of my fault for trying to squeeze in too much at once. I'm lying. Him being an arsehole is still his and will never be my fault. Let's start at the beginning.

I started talking to this guy and he sounded pretty nice. I mean, yes, he lived in Reading, but nobody is perfect, right? Reading is outside the 45-minute ideal dating zone but where else was I going to find the right man for me if I wasn't willing to break a few rules based on my unwillingness to use my Oyster card?

We talked on a Saturday morning whilst I was prepping to go to a concert at a PGA tournament (Mike and the Mechanics; don't ask about it but I'll tell you that we weren't allowed to dance and I almost had an altercation with the 'uncle' security guard). I told him that the PGA thing was in Surrey and it turned out that was not too far from where he lived. I don't have a mental map for anywhere south of London, but I vaguely remember Berkshire and Surrey being neighbours, so I agreed to come over after the gig.

He told me that he was a Methodist with a daughter, had a job and was looking for a good girl. I nodded sagely and said that worked for me whilst I tried to find a 'good-girl' outfit. I mean, what did that even mean? I decided on a harlot red dress which was slightly longer than all my other harlot red dresses because you know what, I was trying.

As I left the gig, I sent him a text to make sure we were still on for a meet at a shopping centre called The Oracle. He took a moment to answer and said that he had to work. Huh? He had been very clear that he worked until 5pm on a Saturday and it had already gone six. I asked him what was going on and he said that he hadn't actually thought I was going to come through.

Exasperated, I blocked him and scrolled through the other options. I was not wasting my harlot red dress on nowt! When I finally got an Uber to pick me up (FYI, golf clubs aren't Uber-map friendly) I got a ping from PoF. It was a dude up for a date that night. I didn't have time to go home first so arranged to meet him in Westfield at 10pm.

Mr PoF had dreads and a bit of hotep about him. Not too much though but I did shiver whenever men called me sistren or their sister. That said he seemed respectful and he was available at short notice. These were good things. I wanted to say that there was chemistry, but I struggled with his accent and found that he didn't listen when I talked unless he'd asked me a direct question like whether or not I lived alone.

I finally got to Westfield and as I was starving immediately started thinking about places to eat. He arrived 20 minutes late which, given he lived 20 minutes away was a bit of a piss take, but I was too tired to waste time on being mad. All my anger had been directed at Methodist in Reading. I told him that I was going to have to eat and he said he would watch me as he'd just eaten. As you can now guess, this was wasteman code for, 'I'm not paying tonight so know it's on you.' Got it.

We went into Busaba (Thai) and I ordered my regular meal. The thing about being a serial dater was that you knew where to go and eat, what was on the menu and what you liked on the menu, so there was no faffing around. He started to tell me about himself and it turned out that he was an entrepreneur. I soon realised that this was code for broke. To confirm that, he told me that he was currently living on a friend's sofa. He told me his business idea and if the truth was to be told, it didn't sound viable to me at all in a 'slow to market entry' type way so I predicted he could still be on that friend's sofa in 18 months.

He started asking me about my living situation so it was clear that he was dating to meet someone who could put him up. A *hobo*-sexual was not what I needed. I thought about my spare room and quickly concluded that it wasn't something that I wanted to give up for any man. I mean, my clothes needed a home, no?

I carried on with my meal and copious drinks and he ordered himself at least three beers. That was fine, I guess. He was keeping me company. The bill came and I paid. He didn't even reach for it and mumbled something about times being tough. Yes, that sofa sounded hella tough.

As he walked me to the station, it was obvious to me that we weren't a match. I didn't want to take on a project when the first thing I would have to do was fix an awful business model. He couldn't even be a client. I didn't work for free and he had no budget, so this was a non-starter for 10.

We got to the station and he tried to invite himself back to my place. I was supposed to presume that this is for sex but I suspected it was so that he could inspect his future abode. Damn that sofa must have been so uncomfortable! He leant in for a kiss and I leant back. He accused me of being shy and chuckled to himself. Err, no. I just didn't want you. He settled for a hug instead and just as I was about to move away, a cheeky butt grab. *Dude, why do you think this is acceptable. Nah Fam, not the one*

Later, he WhatsApped me complete nonsense:

Me: I've enjoyed being single it's true

Him: Yes, I can see that!

Me: Meaning?

Him: Well, you don't seem like you need a man

Me: Nobody should need a man.

Him: A man needs to feel needed

Me: So errr, what would I need you for?

Him: Security… and I'm very loving

This from a dude who was starting a non-viable business, lived on his friend's sofa and tried to go for a cheeky butt feel? I'll pass thanks!

He tried to contact me for the next six months. I think he worked on a schedule as I always heard from him towards the end of the month. Must have been when the rent was due.

Methodist in Reading also texted me now and then to see if we could meet up, but I didn't have another not-so-harlot-red dress in my wardrobe and couldn't be arsed with trekking out of London. It had also become apparent to me that a WhatsApp block meant they could still text you so I had to upgrade to a double block.

It then dawned on me that Dates 12 and 13 weren't actually meant to happen. That Saturday was meant for music only. Lesson learned. Wait, is Reading classified as a city? Let me go check.

Almost Dates: The Married Guy

I've got a bit of a thing against men called Jason. I find them sneaky. They're not of course but there is just something about the name. Maybe it's nightmares from the horror movie. Yes! That must be it because I can't stand the name Freddie either. Sorry to all the Jasons, Damons and Freddies out there. I went on a date with a Damon once and he was actually evil. I dated a Freddie and, again, evil. We could never work. I mean, at this point of my dating journey, I'm clearly lying as I would date just about anyone but, I'd call you *babe* forever.

So Jason came along and was way too complimentary. I'm not beautiful. I do ok. A strong B+. So way too many superlatives and compliments before we'd even spoken on the phone was always suspicious. We texted for half a day then he disappeared. I guess compliments and beauty weren't enough to hold his interest.

A week later, he reappeared, and I asked him if he'd lost a family member or was ill. He claimed nothing like that had happened but when I probed, he confessed that he'd slipped a disc or something in his back and had been out of it… so much so that his thumbs stopped working. I was already over it. I could sniff a married dude a mile off. I asked him if he was married and he disappeared again. I guess I got my answer.

Let's move on…

Date 14: English Teacher Go Home

When I started talking to this one, I liked the fact that he was an English teacher. I also liked his strange, nearly alien-like bone structure – high cheek bones, angular jaw – it all worked. He was also tall so even if he took off a couple of inches, he was well over 6 feet. So we chatted a little over a sunny long weekend and agreed to meet on the Bank Holiday Monday.

I had made the journey across to the Stratford Westfield as opposed to my local one in Shepherd's Bush because it was closer to him. I tried not to judge this lack of chivalry as a lot of people have a lazy approach to dating and I was trying to be a feminist that day. This hadn't stopped me from wearing unnecessarily high heels that I could barely walk in. By unnecessarily, I meant more than two inches. I did look cute though and as I half-slid half-walked up to Balans, I was actually rather pleased that I got there before him. Nobody needed to see a tom boy walking in heels through Westfield looking for a Balans. Nobody.

I arrived at our meeting point and waited. He was late. Did I mention that I really hated tardiness? Oh yes, I did, but let me give you more insight into how much I hated it. Lateness is a sin to me. In fact the 11th commandment should be, 'Thou shalt not be late'. Like seriously, never.

He sent me a message saying that he was 10 minutes away and sounded really annoyed that he couldn't find the place. I was really annoyed that he was late but, no, I'd told myself to suck it up and see what he was actually like. Eleven dates in and I was starting to wonder if it was me. It wasn't but the thought crossed my mind.

I got the run around for 25 minutes before he turned up by which time I'd nearly frozen to death, so was now inside Balans with a pot of fresh mint tea and a scowl. He walked in and immediately I knew it wasn't going to work. He was growing an afro but unfortunately his hair was receding, *and* he had the most unusual hairline which made it look like his hair was trying to get away from him. And he was late. Not good.

He joined me and started to tell me all about himself. There were moments when he was quite frankly patronising as he explained to me that English teachers were the hardest working ones and how his job was just all so consuming. I didn't know this and he sneered when I highlighted that all teachers had it hard these days. Not as much as English teachers though apparently. They had to actually read stuff. Didn't they go through the same texts nearly every year though? This dude was also teaching at a college and he was making out that life was really hard. I told him that my current assignment finished at 5 and I didn't think about it until the next day. He told me how qualified he was with scholarships and degrees flowing out of his arse. I nodded – a tight nod at that – as I didn't want to get into a degree/job competition. He would lose.

Turned out he was a complete moany arsehole that day. I wanted to tell him that dating arseholes who didn't ask any questions at all and only wanted to complain about their jobs was hard. But I didn't give up, so I switched onto languages and told him of my ongoing struggle with French lessons. He boldly told me that I needed to immerse myself in the language and then went on to mansplain what immersion was. I glazed over as he regaled me with tales of his wonderful teaching and success students. I was certain that his students found him annoying. *Absolument*

There were two key characteristics about him that also annoyed me. The first was that he didn't ask me any questions. The second was that he was still angry with his soon-to-be ex-wife. This meant that he was technically still married, and he hadn't thought that this information was pertinent to share before we met. He was now telling me all about their problems and how angry he was and why they couldn't work it out and how she didn't feel supported, but he had done everything he could because he was perfect and she was flawed and... once again, I found myself counselling a man I barely knew on a date.

I smiled and pushed on. There had to be something salvageable, so I switched onto the topic of travel and living in different countries. His wife and kid lived overseas as she couldn't handle living with him. I was beginning to see why. This dude was relentless as he told me, yet again, how he tried to do everything for her and yet it was never enough. She had eventually taken the child and gone back to her parents as they were struggling financially on his teacher salary. I found myself defending her actions just to get a word in.

The hovering waiter finally managed to intercept during a rare pause and asked him what he wanted. He ordered water. That made it clear that this was going nowhere. I was really hungry, but I also wanted the date to end because he was essentially either an arsehole or sick. Either way, he wasn't having fun and I had made a decision not to try and fix any more men I wasn't already in a relationship with.

Eventually, I told him he needed therapy. He seemed surprised that I didn't think he was perfect. I think I must have been the only woman after soon-to-be-but-not-quite ex-wife to reveal this to him. He didn't seem to be that bothered about the child except that he was being denied the chance to prove that he was perfect, and that she was flawed.

Then he threw a curve ball just as I was thinking that surely this night had to end. What was the curve ball you ask? He had to leave because his friend was dying in hospital. *Not this shit again,* I thought to myself and I may have rolled my eyes because he insisted on showing me texts from said friend (which had come through when he was running late. Yes, I'm still bitter) in which the friend was saying that she was in hospital. What he had failed to find out about me was that I read quickly and can scan a screen in seconds. I told him she was being discharged so clearly wasn't at death's door. He insisted on calling her.

Called her he did, then and there. It sounded like she said not to worry about it as she was being discharged that day. There was a bit of drama from his end as he tried to convince her to let him see her. From the snippets I could hear, this woman was 60 and was remarkably perky. Then it hit me. Maybe this was his Code Bad Date call and I could be busting out of here earlier than I'd hoped!

I excused myself and slid to the bathroom in my too tight heels, plotting my next move. Move plotted, I headed back to the table to find that he was still on the phone to her. I put on my best sympathetic face and pretended to care as he told me that she was fine but that he was worried about her so was going to go to her house and wait for her to come back.

I finally called over the waiter and asked for my bill. English Teacher sat back and watched me pay. No suggestion that his mineral water should in any way be paid for by him, the person who had drunk it. I then told him that maybe, just maybe he needed to see a therapist. His anger towards his wife and life in general wasn't appropriate for a date and highlighted some issues. I figured it was best I got it off my chest because, it was all just too painful. He claimed that he wasn't angry with her just disgusted and disappointed that she couldn't make something as simple as a marriage and a young baby work without running back to her parents. I sighed and, with the help of the table, helped myself back up onto my heels.

Then it dawned on me. This dude had a saviour complex and wanted to save women from themselves. I didn't need saving so he'd quickly resorted back to saving this woman who was on the phone and who didn't need saving either but was more vulnerable. She was in hospital. She was also too ill to tell him to fuck off and stay his arse at home.

So, we parted ways and I made a resolve then and there to,

1. Never to go to Stratford again as it was too bloody far (Zone 2 my arse) and,
2. More specifically, never to go there for a Balans' date

The place was clearly not for me. We did the shuffle back to the station which was really rather long in heels then did an awkward hug goodbye.

Needless to say, we never spoke again.

When You Trust Your Gut

Chatting to a guy online and he mentions the weather. I'm thrown... #ThisWillNotEndWell #40DayDating #DryAsABoneOverHere

Conversation on apps is important and we all need a little flirtatious banter to get into the mood. I immediately sensed that there would be no foreplay with this one. None. Like fingers straight in, a wiggle and, pow! Dick in and casual dismount two minutes later. My profile does say, 'don't just say hi', 'don't interview me' and 'don't be a misogynist.' So simple.

Arse Dude: Hi Chelsea. Love your pictures. Do you live alone? Where do you live? Do you have kids?

Me: Did you read my profile? I'm not really into the interview thing

Arse Dude: Ok I read it now

Me: Cool

Arse Dude: If you can tell me what you really meant in your profile. In simple English please.

Arse Dude (again): *[verbatim]* I didn't get your for what I asked you I know what mean don't be bothered I was joking or if your asleep we can chat in the afternoon.

I had no idea what he was trying to ask me, but I knew this wasn't going to end well!

This user has been deleted

—♥—

Date 15: The French Hope

I've been studying French for a few years now. Yeah, it's not really a language that seems to stick with me, but I've been told that one sure fire way to improve is to date a native speaker. So imagine my delight when I swiped right on a guy who turned out to be French African. Whoop whoop! I'd dated French before and to be honest I'd always found them to be more respectful when dating. They seemed to understand the dance of love.

The effortlessness with which we arranged our first date surprised me even more. He told me that he would be at Waterstone's Piccadilly early so that I wouldn't be waiting. Eh eh! A man that thinks about me and my needs?

There wasn't a lot of flirting or small talk but by this time, with 14 dates under my belt, I was also getting rather efficient at sorting out a date without doing much WhatsApping. I did find his writing tone a little sharp however and thought that it would be interesting to see if he spoke in the same manner as he wrote. What can I say? Tinder had become a bit of a chore by this point.

Date day arrived and apart from what I had to wear, I didn't have to worry because, as promised, he was at the designated spot before me. Quelle surprise! We sat down to dinner and had a lovely conversation *and*... I must admit that I did fancy him more than his pictures would have suggested that I should. Some people really aren't photogenic and shouldn't take selfies. They just look miserable. He was a lot less acerbic in the flesh and rather funny. I could tell that he was ambitious and loved being a father which I found endearing. Things were finally looking up. Could this be a Tinder turning point? He also smelt really lovely and didn't have an ounce of fat on him. I mean, dude was definitely winning. I couldn't wait to get home and tell everyone on Facebook that the dating curse had finally been lifted. Hallelujah!

The only things that I found disconcerting was that he had sole custody over his children, was Muslim (I'm a Happy Heathen) and that he seemed to spend an awful lot of time with his female cousin. I don't know, a woman has a seventh sense and I suspected that they were a lot more than just kissing cousins. He assured me that he was OK with my being a heathen but that if 'we' were to have children, we would need to consider how they were raised. Err, as heathens. What else? Luckily, I caught him just before Ramadan as he ate and paid the bill (this was the first guy that had paid for dinner; wait, let me go back and check; hold on; yep; first date who'd paid; result).

After the date, he went back to sharp, short messaging and he promised to teach me French. It was all going swimmingly until he invited me over to his place for my French lesson. So that was this? Dating was done and we were straight into the relationship bit? Apparently yes.

He told me that he just didn't have the time to date and that he was going to Paris with the children and his kissing cousin so that Friday was the only time he had free to see me. He didn't understand why I wanted to take it slow and not make love to him right away. I realised that even the nice ones just want to fuck sometimes and I was disappointed. And now I may never understand the subjunctive in French!

Mais, he was not to be my last Frenchie. In fact, he was the first of three. *Beau d'amour dans la maison.* I guess this meant I needed to actually do some homework. I mean who needs a French *boy-ami* anyway?

Me… This woman. I do.

Almost Dates: The Married Guy Part Deux

This one worked in a hospital. I knew this because he kept sending photos of himself in scrubs. I blamed Donald Faison in *Scrubs* for making them look so sexy. He could have worked in asbestos removal for all I know but, as he said he worked in a hospital, so it was. He also looked a lot younger than his Tinder age. I wanted to meet him if only to ask about his skincare regime. He could have easily gotten away with being 30 whilst his profile said 40.

We'd been texting a lot, so I called him when Hot Gym Dude was running late. This was around 8pm but he didn't pick up. Next morning he started on the heavy texting again with no mention of the call. Something told me to ask and I did. Are you married? My guess was yes. Yes. I reckoned he was.

He promptly disappeared and my hunch was right. Married. It was a shame as I'd devised a whole role play involving him in his scrubs and me in a nurse's uniform. Just had to wait for the next one. Yes, it's Donald Faison's fault. Otherwise, I wouldn't have looked twice at this dude.

I heard from him again nine months later. I ignored him seeing as by then, I was over my *Scrubs* role play. Shame because I could just about squeeze into that nurse's uniform… I guess it was too late now.

Why was he still hunting me down nine months later? This dude was clearly married so I blocked him. But then he came in left-centre with a new number at 6am on a Sunday. Dude wasn't right. Was this some universe thing that I wasn't aware of? Was there a planet in retrograde? Did I evoke his energy by writing this chapter last night? When would this nightmare end? Now I was sleep deprived and I didn't even get dick as compensation? Fuck this.

Next!

—♥—

PART 5

Dating Glad

Date 16: Big Hands(ome) Builder

I've had to do a quick date reshuffle because I'm superstitious about numbers. Tonight #Date18 becomes #Date16. #40DayDating

#ILikeHim

OMG so I must confess to liking this one. Apart from the fact that he was Southern African and good with his hands (builder or some such) he totally got my sense of humour. A rare find indeed. Maybe because he was silly and immature with a sexually deviant twist and I can be too. See? Soul mates!

I can't remember how we started speaking on Tinder but the next thing I knew we are back and forth on WhatsApp with him sending me photos in his underwear or with his sister or, just looking cute and happy. I actually believed it was his sister. I loved that he looked happy and carefree in his photos because so many of them looked like they were haunted by memories or wanted to fight you over food. I didn't have that kind of energy.

Yes, my singirls, things were looking up. Besides, 16 was one of my lucky numbers! Ok I had to delay dates 17 and 18 to make sure he was number 16 (numerology matters) but I had a good feeling about this one and I loved a dude who was as into sharing as I was. Not just photos mind you.

I felt the Universe needed all the help it could get. He'd told me about the problems with his ex and their business and relationship split. I feigned sympathy when what I really thought was, *Good.* He was free of any ties with her. No baggage. In my head he was riding a horse like Mel Gibson in *Braveheart* shouting 'Freedom!' Or was that George Michael. I wasn't sure. Oh, he played the guitar. Definitely George Michael then.

He also didn't think I would talk to him after he'd told me what he did for a living. I didn't remember saying anything to him that sounded like I was a work snob. Quite the contrary – I loved the fact that his job was physical, that he worked for himself and that he actually made money doing something he enjoyed. I mean, the way my dating luck had been going there were so many out there that were flat broke that a job or a business were already winning in my book. We agreed to have a date that Friday and he made it a point to tell me that he was coming from a meeting so that I shouldn't huff and puff when he was late.

So, I'm getting ready to meet #Date16 and I'm torn between wet-look leggings or a cute red dress. He'll probably be casual. Which one says wifey, but we can't fuck yet? Dilemma. #40DayDating #HelpMe!

South Bank was the meeting point but because he didn't know it well, he got lost which delayed him even further. But I didn't expect that he would be over an hour late. Meanwhile, there I was in a red dress standing outside a red sign waiting on the guy. Turned out that South Bank was a little-known place for some.

Dude is lost. Who doesn't know South Bank? Sigh #Date16! #40DayDating #IAlmostFeelForHim #ThisWillBeBroughtUpAtEveryArgument

Finally we met outside the Royal Festival Hall and walked to Giraffe who were on last dinner orders. Yes, that's how late he was. By this time I was starving so I ordered loads of food. Luckily this was a menu I was familiar with.

He told me that he'd already eaten at his meeting so wouldn't be joining me, but he happily drank a few beers. I was starting to get that feeling of déjà vu but, no, the conversation was so on point and he was all tactile and flirty and, I was so in the zone. I felt like a red dress wearing harlot corrupting a young'un. At the end of the evening, I decided to go for it and asked him out again. We agreed to a Waterstone's Piccadilly meeting the next day and I was totally walking on air by the time I got home.

He called me when he got in and thus ensued a night of sexting and telephone sex. I'm almost proud to say he came over me in that red dress. Finally dressing smuttily paid off! He knew I had a date the next day, but he wasn't bothered because he said that he knew it wasn't going to be as hot as our date had been. All this from a guy I hadn't even kissed yet. Yes, I'd learned from the mistake with Cute Dad Dude. This was me, taking it slow. Don't judge me! I was finally excited and went straight into intense mode. It's what I do.

The next day, I went on Date 17 with BBZ (more on him and his shenanigans later) and 18 then headed home to get ready for my very first 2nd date since 2015. I was so ready for this. I had to wash the scent of Date 17 off me (I said I'd explain all later) and find the right outfit for a post telephone sex encounter.

I decided on the wet look leggings and a vest top. Casually available was the look I was aiming for.

Now Waterstone's is a regular meeting spot for me. I got up to the 5th floor just as dude called me to tell me that he was running late. Cool. He was always running late, clearly. We pushed it back an hour and I had a chat with my favourite waiter before updating my Facebook.

Nine o' clock came and went and dude still hadn't turned up. We were meant to meet at 7.30pm and had pushed back to 8.30pm. I decided to eff it and order drinks for us both and some food for me. Yes, I am always hungry. I ate and decided that maybe I should call him. I mean, this dude didn't know South Bank and so it was a possibility that he didn't know Waterstone's Piccadilly either. But, no. His phone was off. WhatsApps weren't going through and I guessed he was on the tube from East London to me. I was not even stressing at this point because this came with the territory of those who were always late.

Eventually my favourite waiter had to ask me to leave as the place closed at 10. I went outside and called him again. Then it hit me, this dude wasn't on the tube. He had blocked me! His phone was ringing and ringing but my WhatsApps weren't going through. I spotted a 14 bus back to Chelsea and I just hopped on. His loss as I got an appreciative look from the bus driver. Those wet- look leggings were working their magic just not on the guy I'd hoped for.

Tonight I was subjected to a disappearing act. #Date16 was no longer an option. Jelly Babies night in for me. #40DayDating #Ghosted"

I was woken up at 7am by a very apologetic ghoster telling me some story about losing his phone and only getting it back from his friend that morning. So he was a liar too and clearly didn't understand the tick system on WhatsApp. You see, being a blocker myself, I knew one when I saw one. Anyway, he carried on with his fable.

Apparently, he was in some pub getting drunk when he lost it. I asked him if he lost it down some girl's cleavage and he laughed nervously. So that was it. He got a better offer on the night. A sure thing. That's fine, but why lie? We didn't owe each other much at this point but I would have thought the truth might have been better than this cock and bull story.

He made contact once again after that saying that he was thinking about me, but my heart had long turned cold on him. I knew I couldn't afford to let a liar back in. Shame though. Those hands and that six-pack still haunt me. And google photos kept bringing them up on my phone. Urgh!

By this time I was documenting and sharing my exploits and to be honest it was nice to have people supporting me on my journey. I didn't feel so alone in this dating desert. Yes, some thought I deserved all the bad dates, but most couldn't believe how awful the dating recession was or shared their own experiences which were just as dire. But the thing we all agreed on was that occasionally we all need a Date16 to remind us of why we are bothering. It was a game of two halves and clearly his stamina didn't win him the cup.

OK, enough with the sports analogies. Let's sadly move on. **Pours a little cranberry juice for the soul mate that almost was**

Threesum?

It's not what you're thinking. A random Tinder dude I had been chatting to just sent me five photos of threesums to 'cheer me up' whilst I'm resting and recovering from the disappointment of Date 16. Unsolicited. Just, here, this will cheer you up.

#IHaveQuestions. Why are four out of five all B*ckys? The fifth is of two black women with weaves and no dick to share. Black women don't get a penis to play with? Why do they all feature two women and one man? How would that cheer me up? Two hot dudes might work… I'm digressing. Why all of this before we've even met? Why would he think this would cheer me up?

#40DayDating
#ThisWillNotEndWell
#WhyMeBlackJesu?
#SoManyBloodyQuestions

Married Guy Numero Tres

This one gave good conversation although he did love to disappear. But he always came back on a Monday though.

Me: So why no bio? Are you hiding from a partner or something?

Prick: Haha :D

Prick (again): Oh I never bothered to write one

Me: I see…

Prick: So what do you want to know?

Me: So that's your general attitude to dating? What do you think is imperative that I know?

Prick: What I'm on Tinder for

Me: Go on [Prick]. Don't be a tease. Bare all. Not literally of course

Prick: I'm not looking for a serious relationship. :D

Me: Right so what are you looking for?

Prick: Just someone to spend time with when I'm down here for work. Like this week.

Me: I see. You want a part-timer? Are you married?

Prick: Yes with 2 kids

Me: Figured. The weekend disappearance is a dead giveaway

Prick: Haha… nah I was just really busy… have been for the last few weeks.

Me: Then you don't have time for me lovely.

Prick: I do now dear

Me: Best you find someone also married who won't require more input

Prick: Finished the project yesterday

Me: OK so, thanks but no. Married guys aren't for me. Best of luck though, stay blessed and try not to get caught

Prick: Let's get a drink or dinner sometimes though

Me: Why?

Prick: Because I superliked you and would like to know you

Me: But I'm not going to give you what you want so why waste both our time? I may get superattached and ruin your happy set up. You don't want that fam. I'm not the one. Choose someone who has as much to lose as you. There are sites for this

Prick: Haha… I'm not happily married. I won't be here if I was. So much missing I don't have anything to lose any more :D

Me: Again I ask, has that line ever actually worked? Dude, work on your lines. It's a pity as you're almost cute enough to make me pause and you write in full sentences which is rare but, a married dude with kids who hasn't even dissolved the marriage is too '80s American drama for me. Like *Knots Landing* drama and not even *Dallas* or *Dynasty*. I'm out. Stay blessed xx

Prick: Thanks for making time to talk to me… very kind of you. Take care

All of this for a super like. Imagine what he would have expected if we'd ever met for that drink. I hate men who blame an unhappy marriage for cheating. Leave!

Date 17: BBZ

My concern is that he spells 'babes' as 'BBZ' and 'was' as 'woz'. However, it's mainly that he calls me babes. I mean BBZ.

#40DayDating #DoubtHeIsAFeminist

So I think, as I write this one, that for many different reasons, this may have been my favourite date of them all. Only because I laughed so hard and the sun was shining and the innocence of some is so infectious.

It was a great weekend. At the time of arranging the date I was still riding on the high of Date 16 and looking forward to our second date later that night. Yes, I did think Date 16 had potential boyfriend material written all over that hot body. But I had learned not to put all of my hopes into a penis so was continuing with the dating. I was almost having fun again.

Date 17 was different. No witty repartee or long conversations on the phone. He was cute but looked young. Turned out that he was younger than his Tinder profile suggested but only by a year – 37. We spoke and agreed to do a Sunday lunch in Clapham Junction. I was planning to stick to Revolution bar as I had memorised the menu, but he claimed to be running late and couldn't find it so asked if he could meet at the train station instead. My brothers, Google is not your enemy. I beg you use it!

I walked back to the train station and I kid you not when I tell you that he turned up in his brother's car with brother driving because, I later found out, he wanted to know if I was, a), going to turn up and, b), was worthy of his time. Apparently, I passed the test as his brother sped off in a dim-windowed car. I didn't even get to see him. Drat!

I turned towards BBZ and he was cute, young-looking and had small wrists. I don't know why this unnerved me, but it did. I tell him we're off to Revolution. So off we went and soon as we got there, settled into our table. He looked at the menu and started to back away. It was a beautiful day and I figured it was because he wanted a table outside. But oh no. It turned out that the dramatics were because he didn't eat English food. Just Caribbean or West African. I gave him one long look. He couldn't have mentioned this before now? And what's with these staunch 'No English food' guys? Yes English food can be bland but… anyway again, I digress. Back to BBZ.

He then said he was willing to experiment. I suggested Buona Sera, an Italian place and his eyes sparked up again. I started to look around for street cameras as, clearly, I was being punked. Who had not had Italian food before? Where did this one come?

He didn't know what poached eggs were, but he wanted to try something different. So Italian…

#WantsToExploreLifeOneEuropeanRestaurantAtATime
#ThisWillNotEndWell

But there was something really sweet about him and I was a sucker for innocent guys who weren't just trying to get their leg over. Or so I thought.

We had some weird conversations including one about diets. In it, I mentioned the blood type diet. Not that I'd ever done it, but this was me trying to make light conversation. He didn't know that there were different blood types and stared at me in fascination as I enlightened him. I mean, how do you not know? He's got kids. How is this life?

He seemed overly impressed that I read books and confessed that he had never read a book in his life. Like, seriously, never? He looked so grave as he said that he would read books for me though. I had to suppress laughter because the sincerity was so touching. I wondered if he could read but thought better than to ask.

Anyway, it turned out that he was a barber, lived with his brother and was trying to save for a place of his own. This then turned out to be a council or housing association place because he realised that his self-described *likkle* pocket change was never, ever going to be enough for a whole place for one in London.

I haven't laughed as much as I did with BBZ although it was more *at* him instead of *with* him. His innocence and naivety had me in unsuppressed tears. His bum obsession… not so much. He talked openly and freely about this butt obsession of his and told me that mine was the reason he'd gotten out of the car in the first place. I tried to distract him with talk of anything other than my arse to no avail.

I then noticed that as we ate our pasta (which he loved by the way; sea food linguine will always remind me of him) he kept looking at my hair and I thought, Oh, *here we go with the hair critique*. Finally, he asked me why I shaved the sides. I told him I had alopecia. With a confused expression, he asked me what that was? I was sitting there thinking, *Fam, aren't you a barber? Surely, you've come across alopecia.* I gave him the benefit of the doubt though because it's not as common in men. After I'd gently mansplained it, he said that he had heard of it even though his confused look remained. I was guessing this was the first time. Bless. Then he turned all pensive which looked like it hurt and said, "BBZ, six months with me and your hair will grow back." He was so serious I burst out laughing.

That's when it hit me. He had to be a weed-head or his mother had dropped him when he was a baby. That was the only explanation for this level of ignorance. I mean he wasn't even offended by my mansplaining. For the right woman he would have been such a gem but, as I paid for the bill (I know, but he's saving for rent and the numbers on the receipt made him shudder a bit), I realised that he probably wasn't the right one for me. Shame as I'd enjoyed laughing. He was cute though. Cuter than Cute Dad. And all that sexting with Date 16 had put me in the mood. Hmmm...

One thing though. He threw me off course with a disproportionate amount of anger towards his daughter's mom but then, this wasn't new. It just didn't seem to fit in with the rest of his guileless, simple personality. Hmm...

As we left the restaurant, he suggested that we go to a local park and hang out. I had some time to kill before my rendezvous with Date18, so figured why not enjoy the sunshine? And so the making out began, in a park in Battersea with my clothes on. I'd missed this careless disregard for the norms and just enjoying being alive. It was the right date at the right time. I just wish it was with Date 16 and not Date 17. See, I told you numbers were important.

All that making out meant I was in danger of running late so had to go. He wasn't really having it and offered to come with me. On another date. He said he didn't care and that after that we could go back to his and hang out. Errr, no. Why would he think that was an option when I'd told him that I had other plans for my evening? What was he going to do? Get his brother to drop him off again? I was wary about people coming to my place at the best of times and, it turned out, this time it was for good reason.

Turns out BBZ wasn't as innocent or as sweet as I'd first thought.

Chatting to Dude on Tinder

Dude on Tinder asks me what I'd done today. Normally I'd be honest and say, "Watched porn, eaten chocolate and passed out again twice," but I feel this may lead us down a freaky path I don't really want to go down. So, I say, "I was catching up with friends and chilling." #WheresTheLie #40DayDating"

He writes in French I write back in English. So he asks me if I have children and I say no. You? He gives me some long, convoluted response and his phone number without answering. I take it to mean it's complicated.

It wouldn't have worked anyway. He's a *sommelier* and I'm allergic to wine. He also mansplains his job because he clearly thinks I wouldn't understand or don't know about Google...

I'm trying but the way my brain side-eyes those who avoid questions but mansplain, I have no time for. #40DayDating #10DatesToGo #SorryNotSorry

Let's get back to BBZ.

Date 17: BBZ Part 2

What I initially liked about BBZ was that he understood when I explained things to him. Like as we walked back to Clapham Junction, I explained how we could never date because we weren't a match and although there was a physical attraction that wasn't what I was looking for right now. We parted amicably and I smiled as I rushed over to Waterstones and Green Park to meet Date 18. I was getting a case of the déjà vu but with having done a double before a treble dating day, it didn't stress me. I could handle it.

As I was on #Date18 in another park *sans* the kissing, I noticed that I had WhatsApps from BBZ and who was really horny. I got it. A snogfest in the park on a sunny day was fun. But seriously, I'd already moved on. We had agreed that we weren't a match. Some of you may argue that I'd led him on by kissing him, but I don't really think that was the case. He knew the deal as I'd been very clear. I mean, how was he in the business of hair yet didn't know the basics of alopecia? This dude had *me* all confused. Weed is evil y'all. Just say no. And that's exactly what I had decided to do with BBZ. But BBZ wasn't going without a fight.

All I could do was lie and say that I was meeting friends. Date 18 was sort of a new friend, right? Then BBZ wanted ice cream. I should have told him that I was lactose intolerant, but he probably wouldn't have understood. And I didn't have the time or energy to explain it. Yes, I was already thinking about what he would and wouldn't understand. How sad was that? Then followed a barrage of sexual messages with aubergines and horny devils.

BBZ: Hey

BBZ: What are u doing

BBZ: I know u r with friends

Me: Yes

BBZ: Wanna lick up like ice cream

BBZ: Take you to ecstasy

So this was the situation. Though not very bright, he was harmless but, I couldn't risk it. Even though the kissing wasn't all that bad, I couldn't even shag him because then he would know where I lived. Safety first. Besides, I was suspicious of the fact that he couldn't take no for an answer and was still angry at his baby mamma even though baby was now a teenager. Persistence and anger are kind of turn offs for me. I couldn't trust someone who had no control over his actions and emotions. Too unstable. I decided to just ignore him. Yes, I decided that that would work though he carried on.

BBZ: I haven't been to that restaurant before

Me: Yes, I got that

BBZ: I liked the mini octopus things [calamari]

BBZ : Delicious

BBZ: I wanna caress and undress u ... and show u what I can do

Me: BBZ, it's not an audition

BBZ: I can do a portrait of u in the nude

BBZ: I'm a good artist (dick emoji)

BBZ: *[sends a photo of a zebra]* I want u to sit on me face

Me: Are you suggesting I sit on a zebra? Why are you speaking in song lyrics?

BBZ: Lol

BBZ: I want u to sit on me

BBZ: On my lips. Just me n u

Me: OK thank you for the clarification. You crack me up

BBZ: I wanna be your nasty man. We can become whatever we wanna be

BBZ: I know we r not an instant match. But I'll make u a match I u give me a chance

BBZ: Not an instant match intellectually. But we are in another department

Me: Yes intellectually we aren't a match BBZ

Then he started asking for nudes so that he could draw me. I don't get all of these artists and photographers out there trying to get nude pictures of everyone. It's not sexy. Stop it. Stop offering to draw me in the nude. I don't want it thanks. And who are these women craving being drawn and immortalized on dates? I beg you also stop. Now guys are selling their pre-GCSE art skills for sex.

Now he was giving me so much joke that I was loathe to let him go. It was all harmless. Right? Hallelujah! He got it. We didn't have to play this game anymore. I was free. And then the next morning I got this:

BBZ: *[sends two auburgine emojis]* He wants u

Me: Who is he?

BBZ: My precious tool.

BBZ: That would hit your g spot

BBZ: Like a pornstar

Me: Eye roll emoji

BBZ: Have you ever done a 69?

BBZ: Maybe I shouldn't have asked you that. Sorry.

So, sitting on his face with talk of his aubergine were fine but numbers, no. Sadly by this point, it was clear that I couldn't shag him. Sigh. But… it kept going on and on with the random WhatsApps. I was quickly getting tired so went back to straight ignoring him. Then he finally seemed to get it and for that, I was pleased. He was initially so gracious, then he went and ruined it. He still made me laugh, mind you. There was a naïveté to him that was endearing. But no, not long-term potential. I could however see how some women would be OK with it.

But I kid you not when I tell you that… BBZ came back again. He just wasn't hearing no. And what's with guys and spanking? They think it sounds dominant and sexy, but it just sounds sleazy and painful. By this point, I was beyond exhausted at having to guide him through a rejection. I mean, surely this wasn't the first time he'd heard no?

BBZ: If you aren't interested then there isn't much I can say that will make you interested.

BBZ: So I'll just have to say goodbye

Me: Exactly. Glad you understand. Take care and stay blessed!

Next day whilst I'm at work:

BBZ: I wanna spank u

BBZ: LOL. In my dreamz. I know you don't like me

BBZ: Wow I really wanna kiss you up

BBZ: You would love to be in a dark place with me. It would be good for you

Then the following day:

BBZ: Why are u not saying anything?

BBZ: I would like to see u again if that's alright with u

Me: BBZ we aren't a match. I don't want to waste your time or your energy. And I told you I was ignoring your messages. Go find someone who wants you for you and thinks you're amazing. I think you're cute and sexy but that's not enough

BBZ: But why not? I think we had a connection

Me: Because it's really not going to happen. Just accept my decision with the grace I know you are capable of demonstrating.

Then the next day:

BBZ: So how about we have a one-night stand before we say goodbye.

Me: Joker. Cute offer but no

BBZ: Oh well, at least I tried

Me: You really did, and I'm flattered

I think it's fair to say that he's the one that I miss the most because he made me laugh so much and there's nothing sexier than a man who can make you laugh. Except maybe a man who can make you feel and think and dream. I wish him all the best and know there is someone out there for him and his weed-loving self. It's just not me.

—♥—

Date 18: The Mature Student

When you tell a dude to share his fantasy hoping for decent phone sex then it turns out that he's got fantasies of becoming a delusional dictator of an African country and doesn't believe in feminism. I don't see how he can unsay these things... #40DayDating #ItWasAllANightmare

As you may be able to tell by now, I'm a sucker for an intelligent guy. I honestly don't care about looks if he can turn me on with words. So this one had great photos. He was tall, East African (which was a nice change), a shy smile and did I mention tall? Ok, maybe I'm a little superficial with the physicality. What can I say, I like height? It allows me to be less self-conscious about my horizontally-challenged self.

He told me that he already had his degree in something completely vocational but that he wanted to study a masters in something humanitarian so that he could go back home and help his people. After a couple of conversations on the phone where I found his accent and motives completely adorable, we agreed to a meet. This was one of my busier dating periods and I had three dates booked for one day. I know, I don't know why I thought this was a good idea, but I figured I could make it work. I mean East Africa isn't *that* far if he did go home and save the world, right?

Yes, initially he didn't mention the child he had but I sensed that not all was well with him and the mother of the child. I didn't take this as a lie, more an omission. By this time I was starting to get the business idea of starting a support group for men with anger and resentment issues towards their co-parents and exes. There was definitely a market for it in London alone.

We agreed to meet at my bookshop stop. I got there late because BBZ wouldn't let me get up from the park grass without yet another series of snogs. Date 18 didn't seem to mind and had chosen one of my favourite tables. I immediately spotted those awful Jesus sandals that uncles wear and, dude had big feet. But I told myself that it was summer, and it was better than him wearing smelly trainers, right?

Right off the bat, the conversation was serious despite me trying to keep it light and breezy. His reasoning? He was a serious guy who was serious about life. I then found out that he was not only studying but also working because the mother of his daughter didn't support his dream. I asked him to tell me more about this dream and it turned out that he wanted to be a humanitarian politician. I jested that such a person had to be an oxymoron and that it was like being a vegetarian cannibal. Needless to say, I chuckled alone as I popped a sweet potato fry into my mouth. Fuck him. My joke was cute.

We got back onto the serious topic of saving the world and I slowly began to realise that he was planning to do this purely through studying and amassing degrees – he had two already. He did not belong to any relevant organisation. It had to be done slowly because he didn't have the funds and didn't want to work until he had the three degrees. I want to make a music quip here but after the cannibalism joke fell flat…

I tried to silently roll my eyes because there was nothing worse than a perpetual student. Dude was in his 40s and had spent the last 20 years in and out of university like some sort of jail bird hopping in and out of prison.. Nah. Not for me fam.

By now I was 'all serioused out' so I suggested a walk in Green Park for some air and sunshine and he agreed. I was hoping the sun would lighten his mood but, no, on the way there he told me about his corns and that's why he was wearing those uncle-awful sandals. I nodded in what I hoped was a sympathetic way but, it wasn't enough. We got to the park and he stuck said feet in my face and talked me through each corn like they were his children. I was feeling queasy. My day out in London was now way off kilter.

After BBZ, my brain wasn't really geared up for academic debate. Everything was a critical analysis from the tea to the history of the park. I told him I was only there for the sunshine and company. He kept saying that we would park this discussion and that discussion and then come back to them later. The confidence that there would be a second date was both premature and based on no actual evidence. No wonder this dude was still a student. His research methodology was shoddy… at best.

He then decided to give our date the kiss of death by asking me if I was one of those radical feminists. Before I had time to answer he mansplained that all feminists were radical and that it was feminism that divided the black community. I told him that his analysis of feminism was basically flawed and quite insulting. I realised it was time I started looking for my bus stop. This was now all very boring and my BBZ buzz had completely gone.

Strangely enough, he texted me later that day to tell me that he'd had a good time and could see us working. I had figured out that he was broke, would be studying for at least another six years at the rate he was going and didn't get how unsexy corns were on a first date.

Needless to say, we didn't go out again. I hate corns.

PART 6

Dating The Sad

21 Common but Unhelpful Statements From Friends and Family When You're Dating

So, one thing I've not been short of during my dating journey is tonnes of unsolicited advice from dates, frenemies and well-meaning friends.

1. You're too fussy (code for 'You need to date white guys').
2. You're picking the wrong men (code for 'You need to date white guys').
3. Be more open (code for 'You need to date white guys').
4. You're aiming too high (code for 'You're not all that').
5. You're aiming too low (code for 'We're not that desperate yet. Well we are but can we pretend we aren't?').
6. You obviously don't know what you want.
7. Your list must be too long. Nobody will ever meet your requirements.

8. You're not ready.
9. You need to go out more.
10. You need to go to church.
11. Online isn't going to work for you.
12. You now just simply need to settle with the first tolerable man you meet.
13. Aren't you worried you'll end up alone?
14. You're not getting any younger you know.
15. I can't believe you're single. You crazy or something? (*nervous laugh*)
16. Something must be wrong with you. It can't all be them.
17. Girl, you know you ain't easy. Maybe if you just didn't show them your feisty side…
18. Lie until you've nabbed him. By then it's too late.
19. Just sperm bank! You can be a single mum (apparently that's a dream I should want for myself)
20. Wear something wifey and straighten your hair.
21. Bitch, get a cat/dog. They'll love you.

My Responses to Said Unhelpful Advice

Fuck all of y'all.

I'm good thanks.

He's coming.

I'm ready.

He's just late. We'll fight about it when he gets here then we'll have incredible make up sex and cute babies.

So fuck you but, thanks for your unsolicited comments.

I'll keep on keeping on.

And stop telling me to date white guys.

Almost Dates: His Name was Bills...

B*ills Dude*: So where do you live?

Me: Fulham Area

Bills Dude: Niiiice

Me: You?

Bills Dude: Hackney

Me: Niiice

Bills Dude: ??

Me: I thought we were complimenting each other on our areas.

Bills Dude: What do you do

Me: Try to explain the complicated work-shy self-employed mess that is me in less than ten words. You?

Bills Dude: I'm a part time catering assistant

Me: OK. Are you studying too? *[God, please not another bloody student]*

Bills Dude: No

Me: Is that what you love doing? Working with food?

Bills Dude: No. but it pays the bills

Me: So what did you study?

Bills Dude: construction

Me: It's all creative, right? No other job

Bills Dude: No

Bills Dude: So you live alone

Me: Nope.

Bills Dude: Children

Me: Nope. I have a lot of pets. And spirits.

Bills Dude: I live alone. Wanna come to Hackney

Me: Now?

Bills Dude: Yes

Me: No

[2-hour silence]

Me: So we are done here right?

Bills Dude: When can we meet up?

Me: For what, we are clearly not a match.

Bills Dude: Then unmatch me then

Me: *[Unmatches]*

Now I'll never know what his bills were that allowed him to work part-time as a catering assistant. Neither will I see Hackney by night *[fake sad sigh]*.

Almost Dates: The Barking Tolk

Dude: Hi… How u doing… Hii

Me: Hey. How are you?

Dude: I see I'm OK thanks. Where abouts in London r u

Me: Erm… No small talk I see. Chelsea

Dude: OK cool have you got kids and what do you do for a leaving. I'm in Barking *[I hate Barking. Too far]*

Me: In my profile it says I hate being interviewed. Clearly you didn't read it or you just ignored it because you know best. This isn't going to work

Dude: I was just trying to get to know you that's all. The easiest myght be to have a coffee and tolk if that's OK with you

Me: No I don't think so. We're already quite different. Good luck and stay blessed.

Dude: Ok cool

Date 19: The Ex-Vegan European Breast Lover

I'm not going to lie, after the disappointment of Date 16 I was waning. Small talk was exhausting, and I'd gone right across the spectrum from one who could possibly qualify for benefits by virtue of his mild learning disabilities to another who thought he should be running African Mensa… in sandals.

I didn't know a lot about this one as his messages were very succinct. Honestly? I hadn't had a lot of time as I'd juggled five to eight guys that week. So it was my fault. I hadn't done my due diligence.

We met at Embankment and surprise, surprise, he was running late. Not too late thankfully and his short messages suggested that he was on his way, yet he didn't seem too apologetic about it either. When he did finally arrive, he looked… different. He had an afro but was *so* skinny. I looked at him and I was sure people would think I was escorting my nephew. I'm sure I'd set 35 as my lowest age. This dude was a liar. He hadn't seen 30 yet. I bet he couldn't even grow a beard, nor did he have pubes. Sigh. At least he was the last one that weekend, then I could go home and back to sulking over Date 16.

I tried to make conversation but apparently his messages were a true reflection of a quiet nature. This was however bordering on being rude. I mean, why be on a date if you didn't want to talk? I knew that there was no chemistry, but I was hungry.

I asked him what he fancied eating and he said that he didn't care but that he used to be a vegan so anything really. I think he saw the look of sheer horror on my meat-loving face as he assured me that it was only for a year. Letting out a relieved sigh, I took him to Nando's in Covent Garden. Like I said, I was hungry.

After I witnessed a Nando's virgin place his order (sigh, what black guy in London do you know that doesn't know how Nando's works?) I realised that my instincts were indeed correct. He wasn't a match.

He told me that he only dated white women but that his mum wanted him to try something different so he thought I would do. So, I, Chelsea Black, was an experiment in black dating. I gave him the universal raised eyebrow that said, 'Oh?' which meant that he should stop right there. Clearly, he didn't understand the universal language as he proceeded to tell me about Black women and how he was into white breast meat. He loved Eastern Europeans and the last two girlfriends were from some newly created countries that I didn't care to visit. He had even started learning Serbian or something.

By this point I'd stopped the 'eating with my utensils' thing. I didn't care what he thought of me and he clearly didn't care what I thought of him. So I politely asked him why he thought he was single. He said it was because he had unusual sexual tastes and a lot of women couldn't handle it. He hinted at some regressive role-play and some pegging stuff and I thanked the business model gods that

Nando's was a pay first establishment. I told him submissive was just lazy but trusting and he looked at my 32D breasts like they couldn't nanny him the way that he needed. This wasn't going to work. I needed to be at least a G cup.

This child was a classic timewaster and didn't even pay for his veggie pitta thing. Needless to say, after we'd said our goodbyes, we never contacted each other again. It's fair to say that as a Nando's date he was probably the worst. And I still paid. This wasn't the 'breast' match ever.

I was now officially exhausted by my dating hat trick.

PART 7

Bitter Dating

Date 20: Bitter Blood

Shit! I forgot to do my 100 swipes before bed.

97, 98, 99, 100! Tinder Tactics #40DayDating

This dude had two names, so I swiped on him twice. It was all a bit of a mess as my administration was now really way out of hand.

After this debacle, I did decide to limit my Tindering to mornings and evenings. Daytime Tindering whilst at work wasn't really working for me. I needed to treat it like I would a job or exercise regime. It somewhat saddened me though that dating had become such a structured process, but nobody can understand how overwhelming it can be. I needed to have a life outside of dating. I wanted to shout out to all of the men who made the effort with their profiles. To those that had more than just a photo on their dating profile. Or more than one dating profile. Then again, I was still judging them on three seconds of interaction so, who was I to talk?

Back to the date. He was in his late 30s and hadn't been in the UK that long, he said. Turned out that he had lived here for over 20 years which was more than half his life. He had children but said that he wanted more as it was his way of paying back to society. I thought that was weird, but I also thought it was a clever way of not talking about his children. Fair enough.

We chatted more and agreed to meet in Balham which was on my way home from work. Not that I'd ever really been there. He said that worked for him. So why was he 25 minutes late? I started to think that maybe Frenchie and his 'no-dating self' had a point. I mean, yes, it's summer but I needed to get home and chill after a day at the plantation.

He finally arrived on one of those fold-up bikes huffing and puffing like he was going for the yellow jersey in the Tour de France. I wouldn't have minded if he'd just told me that it was going to be a smelly date. He was cute but I was distracted by his sweating. There was just so much of it everywhere. He went in for a hug and I winced as we made physical contact. This didn't bode well. I have an aversion to sweaters.

I suggested that we go to Electric Cinema for a bite to eat as it was the only place I knew in Balham. I know, Balham may as well be the Bermuda Triangle as far as I was concerned. I had no idea what was where or how to get in or out. And after this date, may it forever remain a mystery. Read on to understand why...

By the time we reached the cinema, I realised that a whole dinner with this dude was going to be tough. To start things off, he said that he wasn't that hungry. So, cheap as well as sweaty. We got to the cinema bar and restaurant where he spent ages looking for the ideal spot to leave his fold-away bike. He then said he was going to the bathroom to change. Oh? A costume change on date one? This was different. I hoped he would come back smelling a little fresher but, no. It was the same stench. I'm sorry my singirls, I have a sensitive nose.

He's cute but the jeans are too tight. You're struggling to walk fam. No. #Dealbreakers #LetOurFutureKidsHaveLife #40DayDating #OntoTheNextOne

Then the monologue started. He worked in the blood-taking NHS industry and had gotten some woman to buy him a degree in some random science subject. Huh? Why was he telling me this? He then went on to tell me how when he had first arrived in the UK, he had rinsed a series of white women for money, contacts, etc., and that's how he was where he was today. I asked him where he was exactly, and he gave me some sob story about immigration woes and accommodation drama courtesy of these women. But then he said that they had all suddenly turned on him. He was *so bitter*. I figured the moment the women realised that he was using them, they rightfully ran for the hills.

He didn't see it that way. As far as he was concerned, they'd used him for his body and then left when he asked for more and more stuff that they were no longer prepared to give away for nothing in return anymore. They'd housed, fed and educated him but he was the victim. It all sounded very transactional and narcissistic.

Then it hit me. All of those questions about where I lived were yet another way to find out if he could find a new home. Luckily, I hadn't ordered any food. This was not going to work for either of us. I hate taking care of broke men. Hate it. Why take on a project when I'm enough of a project as it is.

I suddenly developed a headache as he suggested another cranberry juice, so we parted ways. He looked disappointed as he realised, he and his fold-up would not have a new parking spot. I was just relieved to get away from his sweaty body and constant moaning about how women had done him wrong. So a bloody no from me for the blood worker.

Date 21: Bitter Divorce

Just when I thought a man couldn't be more bitter, I met Mr Bitter Divorce. Let's just say there is nothing more off putting than to sit across a man who is still angry with his ex-wife for what turns out to be not a lot. Let's delve deeper…

Another Tinder swipe and I'm not going to lie, this one was hot, hot, hot! Not quite as hot as Hot Gym Dude but he was still a whole special kinda coffee mocha chocolate male. Sorry, I need a minute.

OK. I've pulled myself together.

He lived far away (Romford? Rotherham? Rotherhithe? It started with a Ro) but needed to come near me for work, so we decided to meet at my local VQ for a late dinner. I think he did one of those rail track-related night jobs. I can't be sure as I lose the will to live when men are mansplaining their technical jobs. He turned up only ten minutes late and we ordered our food. As he was

Nigerian, I already felt comfortable with some of his humour. Sadly, there wasn't much of it on our date.

I suggested an alcoholic beverage for him and that's where the date took a weird turn. It turns out that he'd developed a bit of a drinking problem since the divorce. He would apparently drink a whole bottle of brandy a night and had lost so much money that he had to move out of his home and into rented accommodation. I suspected that there may have been drugs involved as well but didn't really want to get into a counselling session with him. I mean, chances were, I was going to pay for my own food. There was no way he was going to get coaching or counselling for free too.

As he spoke, he did the LL Cool J lip-licking thing. At first, I thought it was a sexually suggestive move but, with hindsight, I think it was an alcoholic licking his lips at what he may have thought was Vodka cranberry juice. Bless, it was just cranberry.

Anyway, it soon became clear that he wasn't over the divorce and resented any time spent away from his children because he was such an amazing father (his words) and husband. I sat there thinking how dare he ruin VQ for me. I mean seriously, how am I sitting here listening to how evil he thinks his ex-wife is when all she had done was decide that she didn't want to be with him anymore? There was no cheating. She hadn't stopped him from seeing his children, there was no quibbling over money… he just turned to drink and blamed her for his alcoholism? This guy wasn't on a date, he was at a pity party. Quickly he turned from hot hot, hot to a sad drip, drip, drip. The date ended quickly.

Afterwards, he tried to keep in contact, but every time we spoke, the 'angry-at-the-ex-wife' rants would crop up again. Then there was the time he was driving past my house (how did he know where I lived?) and tried to invite himself around. Eventually, I told him that I didn't think he was over his ex. He seems genuinely shocked by this and told me that I didn't have a clue what I was talking about. Erm, OK. So I left it at that.

He did text me weeks later, but I suspected he was back on the bottle and just chancing it. Sad really. As a divorced person I get how horrible separating can be, but can't we go back to sharing with friends and family not strangers who don't care yet? First date etiquette states that you shouldn't mention the ex and certainly not if you're bitter! But the denial was strong with this one.

Right, let's hope the next one is happier because even writing about this one is giving me the brandy blues. I'm adding 'no counselling' to the Golden Rules. At least hold it back on the first date. Yes, we are all damaged goods but, why were so many of the men out there also broken?

Date 22: The Portuguese Uber

Another Tinder survivor and I should have known that we weren't really a match from the jump. I think I was distracted by the artistic photos (black and white, ooh-err!) and by the fact that he drove an Uber. I know it sounds weird, but I do have a thing for the chatty repartee that is taxi life as well as free lifts. I'm always getting into philosophical debates on football, marriage, raising kids, the drama of Brexit, etc. It made the time go quicker.

Anyway, I wasn't expecting to see him but then as I was in my French class, he said that he was going to be in South Kensington later and did I want to meet up. I was loathed to do it, but I arranged a second date at VQ that week.

Normally I had a strict rotation for Revolution, Balans, Bill's and VQ. I didn't need any establishment to know how many men I dated so I tried to space my dates out accordingly. Bill's in Westfield were on a once a week special and I always made sure it was on different shifts, so I didn't get the same waiter with the pitying look. Yes, the last one didn't work out. Thanks for noticing.

Anyway, this one had the most perfect skin ever, even in his photos. I had skin envy. Long hair… not for me, but his was at least neat. I could imagine him smelling of cocoa butter and palm oil. In fact I could smell West Africa before we even met. For a full ten out of ten, he turned out to be Portuguese-speaking from West Africa, a tad older than me and was delicious.

I rushed out of French class and ironically took a black cab to VQ because I didn't want to be late and keep him waiting. Turned out that he decided to take on one last job so was late. The downside of being an Uber driver, I guess.

When he walked in, his skin glistened and I gave myself a mental fist pump. This one was all sorts of animalistic majestic gait. I was not upset at all. After he sat down, I noticed that his lips were dry. Like, drier than that sunburned skin you have three weeks after your holiday. Uber dry. Sorry, I couldn't resist. He ordered a drink for himself and sat back talking all the while distressing me with his 'drier-than-a-loofah' lips.

I offered him some lip balm and he looked at it like I'd offered to poison his drink. People are weird about sharing products I guess so didn't push it and looked at anything bar his lips as he talked *at* me. I imagined kissing them and ending up with bleeding lips. Oh, the plight of a working man.

And I meant it when I said he talked *at* me. I loved a chatty man but this one sounded like he'd lived a thousand lives of misery. As he regaled me with stories of three mums and four children and how he kept them all in line, it made me realise that the life of an adult immigrant and a domineering wasteman were not for me. He'd lived hard. No wonder his lips were so dry. He told me that in addition to these four children, he wanted two more and was pleased when he found out I didn't have any. His only proviso was that I would need to ensure that they came to live with him and learn Portuguese. I told him that it didn't sound like he had a lot of space to be honest. Our both imaginary and hypothetical children wouldn't be living anywhere but with me. I mean, he even had us broken up already. WTH?

It became clear quite quickly that we were from different worlds and that culturally we weren't going to mesh. He offered me a lift home but after Cute Dad Dude, I'd learned that it was best if they didn't know where I lived. Safety first, my singirls.

As he drove away and I walked home, I thought, *Wait a minute, he drives an Uber!* He literally has boot and glove compartment space for essentials. He could keep a whole family-sized tub of Vaseline in the car if he wanted! That was the last time we talked. The shiny skin wasn't enough for me to compromise my principles. Lip care also counts for a lot and I can't risk my skin being scratched by lips drier than the Sahara Desert.

Birthday Blessings

Wastemen two weeks before the birthday zone:
Hey, remember me? I'm the guy who dicked you around. Can you forgive me so we can hang out for my birthday and I can get some sex? Come on sweetie. I'll tell you whatever I think you want to hear to make this happen.

Wastemen during the birthday zone:
Hello! I'm a human too you know. Why are you holding a grudge? Can't a man lie/cheat/fuckboi a few times without you catching attitude? Wow... Oh come on, just give me a BJ/threesum/doggy-style sex and we're square? You owe me that at least.

Wastemen after the birthday zone:
Well fuck you then bitch. I never wanted you anyway. No wonder you're single.

Moral of the story? Stay away from petty penis wastemen just before their birthdays. #FuckHim #NahFam

PART 8

Dating's Not So Bad

Date 23: French Faith

After the string of bitter dates, I think I'd plateaued and took a rather long break. It was getting kinda hard as I'd exhausted most of the men on Tinder and I was no longer on PoF much. I'd just rejected five on the trot because after Date Vegan Breast Dude I really wasn't feeling like taking a chance and was eliminating people brutally. I'd gone to the other end of the extreme and was due diligence mad. You practically had to propose on the spot and show me your bank statements, last three ex-girlfriends and pass a crazy test.

But then, phew!! French Faith came forward and revealed himself. Not literally. I hadn't had any dick pics and I was bloody grateful. French-African, tall, cute… hmmm, maybe I had a type. Perhaps all those French evening classes were about to be put to good use.

It was all going well as I agreed to meet him after work either in Clapham or Balham. But then he started talking to me about him picking me up in Elephant and Castle. Huh? First of all, I don't really do roundabouts. They're confusing and there are way too many exits for my liking. Secondly, it's… Elephant and Castle! I didn't know that place and you weren't even suggesting the Nando's which was the only place there that I did know. In fact, he was *very* quiet when it came to food. I was about to find out why.

But let's take a moment. Men need to start thinking about our health and safety. We've never met and yet you want me to trek to fucking Elephant & Castle to get into a stranger's car? To go where exactly? This sniffs of Netflix and Chill with a side order of a US-based cop show. I was running dodgy scenarios through my head but then something said to me, *I bet he cancels.*

Turned out that I was so wrong about it all. The dude finally turned up at Clapham… not on time but *early* (these French dudes are hot on the time keeping; I like it) and was waiting for me at Revolution. Unfortunately, it was Ramadan so he couldn't eat. I was like, seriously Universe, *not again*! I was starving!

Instead I took him to the same park Date 17 BBZ had taken me some days earlier. I felt a little bubble of guilt like I was cheating on BBZ but to honest he had gotten so horny and out of hand since our date I didn't owe him anything. We sat in the park and just talked and, for only the third time in the process, I found myself on a date with someone who seemed pretty decent.

Of course, all of this would have been made better if he wasn't fasting and I could have grabbed some sweet potato fries or something. I suffer from the condition known as hangry (angry when hungry) and can't be my usual flirty self on so little fuel.

He'd had an interesting life, was an entrepreneur, very ambitious and all in all Date 20 was lovely and someone I would definitely recommend to someone else. Ex *sous* chef, entrepreneur, French African, 6'1", entrepreneur, lovely energy. Did I mention that he was an entrepreneur?

It would have been nice if he'd mentioned that he was Muslim and that it was Ramadan when I suggested Revolution; mind you this could explain him wanting to pick me up at Elephant and Castle. We talked about his faith and although like the other French guy he said he was OK with me not being Muslim again he'd want the kids to follow the faith. I panicked. I can't do fasting at the best of times and my Heathen loyalty card was my favourite card ever.

I tried to hook him up with a friend of mine, but she was too Christian to consider it. That said, I do believe he was thrown into the mix to restore my faith in men but not enough to make me change religion. I realised that I needed to get my energy back and get this challenge back on track. Anyway, 75% of the way through and I was bound to run low on energy. Faith restored, I moved on and over my dating slump hump.

Speaking of French, a new guy in my class had been trying to talk to me. This week, it was his birthday and had turned 38 with three kids. The week before, he'd told me he was 36 with no kids. Next week… who knows? Either my French is really bad or… faith gone again. Onto Date 24. Encore!

A Two-Hour Chat With Dude...

Dude: Oh before you go to sleep can I ask you one last question?

Me: Go on

Dude: Can I have some feedback?

Me: Feedback on what?

Dude: On how I'm doing. What I could do better?

Me: But we haven't even met yet

Dude: I know but you're talking to others. Maybe you shouldn't have been honest about that.

Me: Hang on. I didn't ask for feedback

Dude: Oh OK. So can I have some? But only good feedback before I go to bed. Massage my ego.

Me: *[silent, but thinking he's a needy, insecure fucker who talks too slowly and plagiarises profiles]* Can I sleep on it?

Dude: Why?

Me: Because I have nothing nice to say right now

Dude: Oh!

Me: Goodnight Dude

Dude: Goodnight Chelsea

#40DayDating

Date 24: Sweaty Politics

So, he was local and if I'm honest I was a little tired of the trek for dates. Sounds lazy I know but you do a two-hour round trip to take an hour to discover that he's not the one. Trying to stay positive in the face of adversity gets harder. That's me. But a walk to a pub was a plan. That is until he suggested Wetherspoons. Should I be worried that he thinks Wetherspoons is an option that will impress me? I'm not 25.

#AWholeMeInThatWholeAwfulPlace?
#ThisIsWhatHappensWhenYouLowerTheAgeRange
#IGaveHimOneLongWhatsAppSideEye

Let me go back. I had decided that maybe my age settings weren't right. I was on the 35-55 range and figured maybe 55 was perhaps too old. So I changed it to 30-48. Don't ask me why but I was starting to feel that maybe 50 was too old for me. But then maybe 34 was too young?

Balancing your searches is one of the key lessons on Tinder. From distance to age it's all so very difficult especially as most people signed up worked in central London and were lying about their age and marital status. Good times. I really needed to find other sources of dates because Tinder was starting to get me down. I think I joined Bumble but that moved slowly.

Anyway, it turned out that this one was also Muslim and on Ramadan. Like seriously, please let me know in advance. Why were we in a pub? It was a late date because he was waiting to break his fast. Weird. I would have been happy postponing it. He was also not based in London and was here to visit his children… and get this – staying with them and their mother. Alarm bells rang as I suspected that he was only interested in sex.

He was a politician back in Africa and didn't want anyone to know his business here. Joker. This one didn't know that we got the *News of the World* and *The Observer* every Sunday when I was growing up. I know what politicians get up to in the bedroom. It's way too kinky for me. He was also a sweater. I love a man who sweats but, only when he is active. We had been sitting down in a half-empty Wetherspoons for 45 minutes and this one looked like he'd run for three London buses. He was also a little too portly for his age. I was starting to think that 34 was his stage age and he was actually closer to my dad's age.

In my mind it was a no and as we walked down the road the constant sweating confirmed this. He seemed to like me, but I didn't do clandestine affairs or kinky sex where CSI have to piece together the evidence only to conclude that he had a fetish. I'm just a vanilla- chocolate-sex chick who wants a man who doesn't have too many secrets. I also didn't think my linen could take that much sweating. I just don't enjoy washing bedding that much.

He wants to meet again… and he called me jovial. I think this is Yoruba for funny with fuck buddy potential as he's close by. And another Muslim on Ramadan? I beg you add this to your profiles!

After this batch of dates, I started asking any potential ones if they were fasting. I can't be hangry. It's not a cute look. I also don't want to die alone in a hotel room from kinky asphyxiation sex. Yes, I know it's a stereotype, but I don't trust politicians. Nobody does and it's for good reason.

—♥—

Dating Age Theory

In my head, I'm still young. I subtract the years of marriage from my age as they don't count. My theory is that my dating age ended with my last marriage and will only start again when I'm in another marriage. That's kind of how it works, right and should keep me in my 20s for a long time. The patriarchal argument is that apparently I only truly exist when I have a man to call my own. Wrong? Ok, so I may be a wee bit older than I imagine I am. But just like celebrities have stage ages (Nicole S, Florence from Florence and the Machines, Jason Derulo being the obvious ones in this field) I have a dating age and so do most of the men on dating apps.

Men seem to fear women who are anywhere near 40 and older. Part of this is because they realise that you've been there and seen all that. You aren't as easily tricked into bullshit unless you're going through a vulnerable phase in your life. The other is that they worry that we are all sperm stealers which will interrupt their freedom and bank balance. Seriously, dudes, stop this. Nobody wants your sperm that badly. If we have spent this much of our lives *not* getting pregnant then the chances are, we are going to be hella fussy about whom we have children with. I'm just saying.

This desperate older woman myth has to be dispelled. Yes, some women have a biological wobble but to be fair this is society's fault. Nobody has the kind of time or impatience to choose sperm badly. And if they are desperate, then chances are they are going to choose someone younger, fitter and with better life prospects than you. Humble yourself and move on.

I also have a theory for how you determine a man's 'dating age' which means his actual level of maturity. I'm rather proud of it as it involves maths and I hate maths. Forget *BODMAS*. Take a man's age, minus 18, divide the remainder by two and add 18. This is his dating age.

e.g., if a man says he's 47 then he is actually 47-18 =29; 29/2 = 14.5+18 = 32.5 years old. So, you will be dealing with the mind of a 32-and-a-half year old in the body of a 47 year old. *Simple.*

However, for the purposes of this book, we shall be using their real ages or, the age they provided. There are in fact three things that men love to lie about: height, dick size and age. The first two by about two inches and the last by about 7-10 years. Don't be afraid to ask for ID if he looks too young (take him to Tesco's to buy alcohol. They're pretty strict on ID) and if you suspect that he's over 60 pretending to be 50, then check his travel pass. Freedom Pass anyone?

None of these things really matter but, lying does. So if you catch him in a lie about something measurable then I say walk away. If he lies about kids or the number of kids then again, get out. A man who is over 18 and can't tell the truth about things that they can easily be caught out on isn't even respecting your intelligence. Get out before you start making excuses like he's insecure or shy. He's not. He's just an arsehole who thinks women are stupid.

How to Know if Age is a Sensitive Subject

An early conversation I had on Tinder:

Aged Dude: Your profile text made me lol. Good morning

Me: Thanks for at least reading it. I see you're into the gym. See I read too

Aged Dude: Yes, I train 3 to 4 times a week, 1 of my businesses is a boxing gym

Me: I'm allergic to the gym. I'm just declaring it now so that you don't think I lied later

Aged Dude: hahahaha

Me: So are you really 36?

Aged Dude: No I'm 26. Why? How young do I look? Where are you from? I'm from West Africa

Me: You look like 46 is a memory. :D I'm teasing. People just aren't always honest about their age on here. No biggie. I'm from Southern Africa

Aged Dude: No a little older

Me: Wait, so you're not 36? 50?

Aged Dude: Explain 'sugar lover'. I see a lot of that on here from women. Do you abuse sugar? Are you fat?

Me: Explain your age. Just means I enjoy eating sugar. I can't comment on all other women on Tinder. We didn't meet and agree to use it as a euphemism for something else.

Me again: I see. You don't want to share your real age, but you're happy asking personal questions?

Aged Dude: Wow yr really uptight

Me: I guess I am. OK well this was short but not so sweet

Aged Dude: I guess yr another one of those angry bla …

This user has been blocked.

Random Conversation Whilst Trying to Tinder

Him: Chelsea, make me your pet. Look after me and make me the man I want to be. Take care of me.

Chelsea: No

Him: Why not? Come on. You can do this.

Chelsea: I know I can do it, but I really don't want to. Thanks for this amazing opportunity 😒 😒 but I'll pass and just do me.

Him: But I'll treat you well! I'll love you really hard.

Chelsea: You should do that anyway. That's kind of the relationship deal

Him: Oh my God! You're so fucking selfish hey. Why do you make everything about you? No wonder you're alone.

Chelsea: OK… well I see there's nowt left to say here. I'm out. Stay blessed, yeah?

Him: Bitch

Chelsea: Pathetic waste man

Him: *[tearful]* you are just so fucking mean!

Chelsea: *[evil chuckle]* If you say so. Bye!

Date 25: Creepy Courier

#Day31 and the countdown has begun. This will be over in ten days. #Date25 tonight. I may squeeze in a double. #40DayDating #FinishLineInSight

This guy was a bit weird from the get go and definitely the most intense. He was a single father of two though, so I kinda understood why he was like that. Intensely protective about his children and who he let into his life.

He said he had gotten with the mother who was Muslim and Middle Eastern. The family had never approved of her getting with a black man and yet they had two children and then she left them… yeah, now that I think about it the story didn't quite make sense.

He told me that he wasn't a timewaster and that he didn't want to date for long so we should see if there was anything there before going forward. I said that suited me and didn't bother telling him that I only had 10 more days of my challenge to go.

I got at least 15 photos of him with his children. Apparently, he didn't have enough on one phone, so he started sending me some from his other number. None of the photos were of him by himself which I commented on but, he persisted. I cooed and asked where to meet? He said he wanted to take things really slow because of the kids. I said cool, cool, so, when? It would have to be in the evening after bed and story time. I stifled a yawn and asked if Wednesday was ok? He said yes and where. He was a courier and was doing a run to Birmingham so needed somewhere he could park. I said that was fine as I think I was travelling myself that day (that was code for I had a date earlier in the evening, but he didn't need to know all that).

We agreed on Bill's in Westfield. It had been at least a week since my last shameful date there so I could face the staff again, right? Looking back this was a busy time for me workwise and I was starting to find dating tiring. So my energy was all over the place and maybe I wasn't delving as deeply before accepting dates. That said, I was having a rare, good day and looking forward to the date. He seemed nice enough to make the effort.

When he took a break from talking about his children's poo cycles (they were both under three) and his live-in nanny, he was a really interesting guy who had lived on three different continents, ran his own business and loved his children. Maybe a little too much information for those of us who don't have children, but this was all a learning curve. Yes, I was having an understanding day. It was not to last.

I got to Bill's, smiled at the young waiter who was doing his university degree in drama (damn, same waiter; sigh) and sat at my favourite table. Dear God, I had a favourite table at a random Bill's. How was this my life?

Twenty minutes later, I WhatsApped him. One tick didn't turn to two then turn blue. I ordered my usual. OMG I was like, really hungry. Something about Ramadan dates meant that I was even more hungry like I too had been forced to fast for… all of four hours. Don't judge me, my singirls. It was a psychological hunger thing.

My meal arrived and I sent another message which again didn't get a blue tick. Then it hit me that I'd been blocked! It was now 45 minutes after we had planned to meet and dude was ignoring me like we hadn't spoken earlier that day.

Then I remembered that I had his other number. I sent him a message and it went through to blue ticks almost immediately. I shat on him from a great height, told him to lose my number on both of his phones and then I blocked him! So there!

#Date25 is a no show and as I use Bill's a lot, I'm going to have to style out my exit. I'm tired. But so hungry. Grrr #40DayDating #Day31 #NotSureTheNand o'sLeftOverIsStillOK"

I finished my dinner trying not to make eye contact with Drama Degree Waiter. It was all so embarrassing. I'd definitely said table for two as well. That was the fastest gluten-free toast and chicken parfait I'd ever had. I paid and headed back out to the train station cursing myself for believing that this one was different.

I started thinking about his set up and the live-in nanny he had with him. It was probably the mysterious missing mum of the two children. I had been duped again! After getting home, I ate some contraband snacks and went to bed.

That weekend, I woke up to a drunken text from him about wanting to be together and something about what he would do to me when he got his hands on me. Why was he drunken texting me at 3.55am after standing me up? Creepy. After my indignation had died down, I realised that as he had blocked me on his first phone, I wasn't able to block him. This was my opportunity to be the bigger person and ask him what was really going on or… blocked! There. That's all sorted. He was now blocked on both of his phones.

Almost Dates – The Security Guard

So this one lived in North London, was studying for an LLB after his divorce and trying to find himself. I thought this was interesting until he started telling me that he had another three degrees that he wasn't using. He was fed up with life here in England and didn't want to do law anymore. I ended up giving him career advice.

There were two things that really annoyed me about him. First, he thought me having a cooked breakfast for dinner was really bizarre. He kept going on about it. At first, I thought he was doing it to get in a few sausage *entendres* but he seemed genuinely shocked. The other was that he asked way too many questions about my finances and how I could afford to live in an area which he deemed too expensive. He then started trying to interrogate my work situation.

Are you looking for a sponsor though, bruv? What's with all the questions about my financial status? We've not even met yet and you are going on like you're credit-checking me. It's obviously a concern for too many men out there. The dating recession is real. He then told me that he was a security guard part-time, lived with flat mates and with that I just knew it wouldn't work. We were in different spaces. Students? Roommates? Nah.

Side note: So far, I had come to realise that Security Guard is often the male equivalent of stripper. Everyone is a bouncer on the side and claiming that's how they get themselves through university. Fees here are expensive. That is a lot of security. Just say you're a male escort and stop playing. We are all grownups.

But the real reason I told him that he wasn't the one is the perpetual student thing. He was talking about all these papers he had to write, and I could tell that this was what he loved. He didn't like work at all and I had doubts that he would ever do more than he ever had to. This was fine but was not a life I could live. I complained about working but I did actually really enjoy it and was even a teensy bit ambitious in a workshy kinda way.

Have a passion but don't settle. I wasn't looking to be anyone's patron.

PART 9

Dating's Mad

Date 26: Fat Shaming Therapy

#Day32 and I'm so exhausted that I fall asleep at 3am and wake just before 6am. I'm not physically fit anymore. One needs to train before a challenge. #40DayDating

I was again starting to feel physically tired and I wasn't sleeping. In turn, I think the disruption to my schedule and the lack of exercise were starting to take their toll. Then I met the therapist. Just what the doctor ordered!

I saw Date 26 on Tinder and I actually thought, *Jackpot.* He was gorgeous! As I'd started talking to him before I had changed my age range, he was over 50 but he didn't look a day over 49. He was a therapist and really into beach photos of his bare chest. I had, up until this point, ignored the obvious gym shots since Hot Gym Dude, but this could work.

We spoke on the phone and the conversation flowed. Before I knew it, two hours had flown by and we were still talking. This felt too good to be true, but I didn't question it too much because I actually felt entitled to a good date. I felt that Tinder and the Universe owed me one. Hadn't I suffered enough? I did wonder why he didn't have any children or ex-wives lurking in the wings, but he said that he didn't, and I had to believe him. I just couldn't figure out what he had been doing with his life?

At one point, he was talking about a wellness event that he wanted to put on and needed therapists. I said I knew a couple, but he said that he didn't want any fat people on the bill. After a ten-minute discussion it turned out that he didn't want anyone with a BMI over 25. It was his event, so I let it go.

He also seemed to think he knew a lot about women's bodies. Clearly, he thought being a therapist made him an expert. He did talk about his business a lot and how he was going to make it big. I asked him what he'd been doing beforehand. It turned out that he had been living a plump, mediocre life like the majority of the rest of the world. One Tony Robbins YouTube video and now he was set to revolutionise wellness. I asked him what wellness was and am still to get a succinct answer.

Black Jesu take the wheel! Date 26 seems lovely but I'm suspicious of 50-year-olds who haven't married or settled and want every woman to be a size bloody 10. #MaybeTooPerfect? #SelfishOrCommitmentphobe?

When we met at Embankment, and as we were saying hello, a good friend of mine turned up. It's so weird when your worlds collide. I think some of my Facebook friends were starting to think the whole challenge was fictional, so it was nice that *someone* actually saw me on a date. I mean, some of my social media friends were shocked that there were so many wastemen out there. I tried to explain what a dating recession was, but most were too busy laughing at my misery. My date didn't seem impressed that I knew people, but I soon found out that nothing impressed him.

We walked over to Benugos in BFI. There, I ordered a cranberry juice and he told me about how much sugar was in it. It was Friday night, and I hadn't even ordered alcohol! I couldn't figure out if he was stingy or just really anal about food. Turns out it was the latter.

I had a slight belly bloat caused by a stressful week of dating. Let me be clear, I'm not fat. My BMI is 26. Same number as this date. But the way this man stared at me like I was the mum from *What's Eating Gilbert Grape* you wouldn't believe. He 'subtly' told me about my sugar intake and how it was ruining my body and making me bloat. He had weight issues.

Now I could see why he was still single. He wanted perfection even though he wasn't perfect. He argued with me when I said that sexual assault was more common than it was actually reported to be. Then we argued more when I said that most women had been on dates with guys who lied. He was now looking at me with disdain. Where was the guy from the long conversations on the phone? This version of him seemed to hate women and fat people. I had too many of both in my circle of family and friends. This couldn't work. Heck, I was planning a number of baby-related fat years myself. Cravings would not be supervised by anyone bar my hormones.

We never spoke again and now cranberry juice leaves a bitter taste in my mind.

Date 27: The Black Scot

I need to give you some background. I'd decided to try and not date anyone called Chris, Andrew, John or Trevor. Don't ask, my singirls. All you need to know is that I'd suffered at the hands and hearts of too many of these men. So I was disappointed when I met a Scottish guy called Trevor.

The good news was that I was nearly at the end of the 40 days and I was looking forward to getting my evenings and weekends back. I was starting to resent having to plan what to wear to work just in case I had an impromptu after-work date.

I had also resorted to keeping hair straighteners and a spare pair of heels at the office behind some old contracts that nobody seemed to bother with. This dating malarkey had turned into a full-time job. I was even carrying my makeup bag around just in case. Nobody should have to live like this. Nobody. Well, at least not a self-confessed tom boy with a flat boots and messy hair fetish.

#Date27 on #Day36. He's short, officious and really into cardio fitness. I'm hoping he's not another fatist.
How can I ask, "Do you have a problem with fat people because some of my family are fat and I plan on some comfortably fat years in the future?" without seeming weird? He's also one of the banned names but I'd arranged this date prior to the ban so he was exempt.
Fingers criss-crossed please although I'm just hoping for decent conversation at this stage. #40DayDating

The whole conversation was over WhatsApp and Tinder, so I didn't realise until we met at Embankment that this guy was Scottish. A black Scot. Cute. He wasn't bad looking but then I knew that from the myriad of photos he had posted of himself in cycling shorts and loose vests. I do like the boldness of men. After an attempt at Gordon's wine bar (no cranberry juice? Erm, nah) we ended up at All Bar One.

So, it turned out that Date 27 was a nearly 50-year-old commitment-phobe masking as a free spirit who was still into his crazy ex who had thrown a shoe at him in Leicester Square last year. He never ever wanted to live with someone and had broken up with three women because they wanted to tie him down after six months. They dared to ask where it was going. Harlots. Enemies of Progress. Evil Witches of the Dating Underworld.

He then told me about men and women and why relationships don't work but sex does. Why he thought that this was a strategy to get me into bed that would work I don't know. Oh, don't get me wrong, I wanted my bed but not with him in it. For a start he honestly came across as damaged goods. Who talked about exes this much? I didn't know how to break this to him, but it was clear that he was flogging a dead horse.

Why was I wasting his time here? Did he not know that despite it all I still believed in love? That I wanted a relationship with someone where we'll laugh and love together. Where there wasn't a doubt that sex would be delicious because we wanted to please each other. Where the worst argument we would have was about who was more selfless and giving. No, he wouldn't know because he hadn't bothered to ask what I wanted. That's right, my singirls, I was still a hopeful romantic; 27 dates in and nobody was about to take that away from me.

After two beers for him and a much too watery cranberry juice for me, we called it quits. There was no chemistry and my vagina had dried up within minutes as he went on about his theories on women and relationships. It was a fail from the time he tried to mansplain men and sex, i.e., men wanted quantity of pussy and never bothered about quality. We wished each other well but maybe it will all hit him when he turned 50. Maybe… dammit I bet he was already 50.

Anyway next up was a young guy in retail with a tongue to die for!

Behave. He spoke six languages.

Date 28: The Smoke Pot

Say no to drugs people. Just say no!

#ZammoWasAWarning #WeedCountsAsADrug

The conversation started off slowly one Thursday night but then the next morning, early, he decided to get really chatty. I did wonder about the random flip in energy levels but maybe he was a morning person.

I already had doubts about our compatibility as I'm definitely a night lass. He was living in some South East part of London I didn't really know of with his mate who owned the place whilst he paid the mortgage on another place in where his ex now lived. I asked if he had children and he disappeared for 20 minutes. Oh dear. Was it a sensitive subject?

Anyway, as I was running for a train he asked if he could call me. I told him in five minutes. I can't waddle and speak on the phone at the same time. Five minutes later, he was on the phone and laughing inappropriately and randomly. Why was he so nervous? In contrast, his texting had been chilled. Then he started talking about weed and how he'd loved it for 35 years. This suggested that he was not the 40 years old that he had put on his profile but rather another child that social services had failed.

He was laughing and talking about weed in between feigned interest in me, but it was all not right. I thought to myself that it must have been some good weed he had burnt that morning. Eventually, I decided to exit as he was not saying much that I wanted to hear.

Smoke Pot: Hope you have a good day at work

Me: Thanks. You seemed a bit out of it this morning?

Smoke Pot: No Chels I'm fine just that I'm relaxed and chilling

Me: Smoking, huh? I hear ya :D

Smoke Pot: No, I don't smoke weed

Me: Oh!

Smoke Pot: How about more sleep lol

Smoke Pot (again): Went to bed at 4am watching movies

Me: Ok

Smoke Pot: So do you live alone or with your family

It was now apparent that he was a crackhead or some other heavy-duty user. It's sad because he worked with vulnerable people and I hoped he was not using whilst they were in his care. Oh, I didn't mention the weird videos he sent, and which took up all my storage which really didn't help either.

Just say no, people. Just say no. I can't do drug users. It's just too much for me. Kinda like dating Geminis – you're dealing with two different personalities.

Date 29: Cultural Exchanges

This is another tale of two dates although to be fair the first one never got off the ground. So basically, I met a guy who worked in retail and spoke six languages. I'm so easily impressed by people who speak more than one language. I think it's based on this 25-year and ongoing struggle with French. I'm not sure. But this was good. I did have reservations about the retail part though because it could just mean I'd be spending more money trying to help him make his monthly sales target. Yes, I had done a fast forward. Once again, I was excited… prematurely so.

We communicated mainly by WhatsApp and I could tell that English wasn't his strongest language, but hey, his English was *loads* better than my French, so he was winning. Some of his turns of phrases were cute. We agreed that he would find a spot for an after work meet on a Tuesday in Victoria.

Tuesday came and he'd forgotten to find the spot. He said that he was willing to come along if I would find somewhere. Err, hello? What's with the lack of effort so early in proceedings? Was this a cultural thing or did he think that as London was my town, I should take the lead? I was already tired of making all the suggestions and to date hadn't had any dates in Victoria. That said, he'd had about a week to ask around.

#NahFam #40DayDating #TooLaidBack #AllYouHadToDoWasGoogleCafesInVictoria

Here's the thing. I had stopped being the organiser as apparently it made them think that I'm paying. Others disappeared because my selection was probably out of their price range. What could I do? This diva could not do Nando's on every first date? Sometimes you just had to splash out and pay a fiver for a coffee. That's the London madness we all lived with.

We got into a debate and he didn't seem to understand why I was pissed off with his lack of prep. All through our exchange I was thinking, *This isn't going to work.* We didn't understand each other. And so I started lining up another date in Clapham. Hey, a girl had to eat, and I didn't fancy running the gauntlet at Waitrose. There was no food in my house at all. Mr Languages accused me of being rude. I accused him of being a prick. This was looking less and less likely to work.

He came back and said we could do Burger King and obviously I told him about himself. I'd never been on a fast-food date as an adult and I wasn't about to start now no matter how hangry I was. It got tense and eventually I told him that it wasn't going to work. He said I had high expectations. I said all he was meant to do was find a place where we could have a coffee. Not Burger King. What I didn't get about this dude was that not only was there a gross lack of effort, but he then proceeded to act all butt hurt when I called him out on his bullshit.

I'm determined to get in another 'stay blessed yeah?' before the challenge ends. Yes, it's petty but I've rarely had the opportunity to say it first.
I nearly did when #Date29 postponed but he wasn't even worth it after trying to suggest a date at Burger King. Eventually we agreed we were not going to be a match. #TeamPetty.

Then I realised that some guys thought that they just had to exist these days and that was enough. This was life on Tinder. Quick access women. We didn't need to do anything else but turn up and expect to be serviced. I yawned at their inability to see that a little bit of effort went a long way in a saturated market. Why not stand out from the bland noise?

I did get my 'stay blessed yeah' in but, it fell flat. As far as passive aggressive kiss offs go, it only seemed to work in English culture. Drat. Time to work on the next one. Surely it was time for a decent date?

Date 30: Mini Dad

This one was a last-minute addition and to be honest it showed. It felt rushed and unfortunately for me he wasn't one to be rushed. Ever!

He worked in social care, was a dad to three kids and Ghanaian. I was hoping that he turned up because he said he was running late and then disappeared on me as he got back to driving. I'd been stood up before as you are well aware… though not in Clapham yet so maybe I was being too pessimistic. Guys seemed to like standing me up in Westfield or Waterstones. Clearly places starting with W were for wastemen. W was evil.

After I got to Revolution, I realised that I didn't know his name! This may have been purposeful though as he had one of those macho screen names that put me off. Like BigDude69 or some shit. Why guys did this I still don't know. Just say your name is Dave or Dele and get on with it. Don't go raising our expectations about your sexual prowess or size.

An hour later and he finally arrived. He wasn't out of breath or anything, but he did say that he wanted to eat elsewhere. He didn't fancy Revolution. This was the third time I'd tried it and guys weren't really feeling it. I blamed the new menu. It wasn't working. So we went up the road to an Indian restaurant. At this point, I regretted two things: wearing 2-inch heels and waiting. He so wasn't worthy of either.

Turned out that he was living with his brother as he was in the middle of a divorce. He still tried to have the three kids every other weekend but there just wasn't enough space for them. He worked far from where he lived and was commuting for hours every day. I think he was tired. And quiet. And short. And he was in the middle of a divorce. These did not make for a winning combination. I wasn't feeling his sexy at all.

I don't know why but he then started to lay in on me for being posh. I'm not posh at all, but his insecurities surely came tumbling out. He was full-on projecting. I couldn't really tell where they'd come from and why he had them. I mean he had a Ghanaian accent, but I was someone who respected an accent. What's with guys telling you about yourself on a first date and then being surprised when you didn't really care to hear whatever it was that they had made up about you?

He tried to tell me a bit about Ghana, but his facts weren't making sense. It did give me a chance to catch his name without asking though. Phew, that could have been awkward. Sadly, he then went on to tell me about South Africa… a country he had never been to, but he'd heard of Nelson Mandela, therefore he knew all about it. Side eye.

I don't remember much else. It was fairly forgettable, and I do recall telling him that he wasn't quite ready to date yet. He didn't have the time or the energy. I suspected that the wife had already moved on and that they were in that competitive stage of divorce where you want to be the one to move on first but, it hadn't worked out for him. I think she won this one.

... And that was more than I was doing. I thanked him politely for the meal (he paid; this was literally unheard of during the #40DayDatingChallenge that it actually has to be mentioned) and he walked me back to the station. I couldn't even see us being friends because he was a quiet person and I would struggle with that. I find myself distrustful of quiet people. Like, share more so that I know what nonsense you are thinking. However, I do recommend the restaurant – if only I could remember the name. It was on Lavender Hill, on the same side of the road as KFC. Look out for it and tell me what you think. And I've forgotten his name. Err...

#Date30 was an hour late and inches short. Mid divorce. He's getting there but not quite ripe. We had a bit of fun though although he called me posh. #relative #40DayDating #Day38

Right, let's try this again, shall we?

Almost Dates: When You Play Yourself Without Getting Any Play

Me: So, I'll be busy for a couple of months

Dude: Oh, what you doing? Work?

Me: Nope. Concert season

Dude: Are you a musician?

Me: No… I told you what I did earlier.

Dude: I don't get it

Me: I just go to lots of concerts.

Dude: Ahhh! So you're like a groupie?

Me: No. Like a fan.

Dude: What's the difference?

Me: Fucking (mansplains difference for five minutes)

Dude: Oh ok. So can I come?

Me: Nope

Dude: Wow. Why not?

Me: Because I just said no fucking. *[chortles at own joke]*

Dude: Ok… so wait. We were going to fuck?

Me: Were being the operative word.

Dude: And now we're not?

Me: Nope

Dude: Why not?

Me: You clearly don't understand me.

Dude: Wait, what did I do?

Me: There you go again acting all confused

Dude: But

Me: Let it go Dude. It's over.

Dude: Wow. Just like that?

Me: Yep. Just like that, groupie.

#40DayDating
#FuckHim
#HeSaidWowThough
#NobodyPutsChelseaInTheGroupieCorner

PART 10

Dating Jack the Lads

Date 31: Wet Wet Wanker

#40DayDating and I'm taking a date to see Wet Wet Wet. #Date31. Let's hope he doesn't take it upon himself to send memes between now and tonight.

Saturday and I was lolling in bed pondering about my life. Just kidding. I was watching porn and more specifically, was trying to figure out how the mother had passed out on what would seem to be only one glass of wine so that her husband could fuck the precocious stepdaughter who had just turned 18. I'm not going to lie. This was how I spent many a morning – dissecting the poorly thought through scripts of porn makers. I didn't think this was a hobby I would ever turn into a job but, I remained hopeful.

Mid-morning, I got a notification from Tinder that a guy I'd swiped right and was messaging. Cute. He lived far though. You know, the part of London nobody goes to? DLR land. I don't understand it and I'm OK with that. Unless it's City Airport, I'm just not interested.

We started chatting and it all seemed good. He asked me what I was doing and instead of being honest and saying watching porn, I told him that I was listening to songs getting ready for the Wet Wet Wet concert that night at Chelsea Hospital. I know. I'm all things cool and rock and roll but to be honest by this stage of the challenge I wasn't bothered enough to lie to people to make myself seem cool. That said I knew porn would be judged so I left that bit out. Baby steps, my singirls.

I was expecting to be dissed for my '80s musical taste but he claimed to love them too. Wow, what were the chances? Slim, right? I told him that I was going with friends of mine but that he was welcome to come along as I had a spare ticket. He said, "What time?" Shit. That meant I had to switch off the porn and go shopping for a new first-date outfit instead. I needed something that said, 'outdoor gig but not too much effort had been made here'.

We agreed to meet at Sloane Square station at 6.30pm. As he was coming from the Outer Hebrides of DLR land, I let him off for being 15 minutes late. We popped into a café for drinks and a bowl of chips. Here's where I started to have doubts. He was happy to order a beer and tell me about his financial struggles. Then he ate my chips. I mean, most of the bowl. When the bill came two beers later, I'd learnt more than anyone needed to about the business of setting up a shoe brand, yet he didn't even offer to throw in a fiver? The whole bill was about £12, and he had beer! This on top of the free ticket and I was already *not* impressed.

He told me how he got into Wet Wet Wet. He said that he was going through his parents' divorce and their music helped pull him through. Fair enough. We all find music in different ways and often through difficult times. Then he went on about how he was not financially ready to date. He was living in a house share after just getting back from dicking about in Asia for some years.

I thought people went there to save money but, I guess he forgot that part. As we walked to the concert venue, I noticed that he was carrying a lot more weight than in his photos. I guess that Asian food really touched the spot and that the photos posted were old. What a surprise.

Once we got to the concert and met up with my friends, the guys immediately bond over a beer. They bought him a beer… and then another. Dude didn't even put his hand in his pocket at any point. Maybe he was waiting for Marti Pellow to hit the long note during 'Temptation' to inspire him. OK, that's what I was waiting for.

Then his behaviour turned strange. Maybe it was the close proximity to a married couple, but he started to get tactile and at one point pinched my cheek. In reality, he pinched the skin that covered my cheek really as I don't have plump cheeks. I think my face showed how unimpressed about it I was. The other thing was that he didn't seem to know any of the songs. Like not a one. Slowly I started to realise that he may not be as ardent a fan as he'd made out. He just elaborately lied in an attempt to bond quickly. And it worked. *Were his parents even divorced*, I wondered.

I asked him which were his favourite songs, and he mumbled something about 'Goodnight Girl'. Google is good oh! Then the phone calls started coming and I could feel his tension as someone called his phone back-to-back. Eventually he couldn't ignore it and said that he needed to speak to his sister. As he left the row of seats, I knew that I wasn't going to see him again. I felt that between his partner calling (sister my arse), not having any money, not knowing *any* songs and me clearly not being as impressed with him as most other women seemed to be, he had run out of stories. I wasn't tempted. No 'Temptation' whatsoever.

But my friend was convinced that he was coming back. I waited and, true to form, he sent a WhatsApp later with some lame excuse about his sister needing him. I tried to remember our call earlier in the day and I don't recall a sister mentioned. But, whatever, the married couple was more annoyed that dude owed them two beers.

I blocked and started scrolling through Tinder just as Marti hit that note in 'Temptation'. I love that long extended note.

Onwards and upwards!

Date 32: Fraud Doesn't Pay

Date 31 disappeared in the middle of the concert to call his 'sister'. The curse has not been lifted. I repeat the curse has *not* been lifted. I need a decent date please Universe. #40DayDating #Fuckeries

The 40 days were over! I wish I could say that I was happy about it but after Wet Wet Wanker, I decided to continue for as long as I could on Tinder because surely, I was one step closer to finding him, no? Then I started flirting and talking to a guy who seemed to have it all. By this I mean a job and a sense of humour. I had been reduced to asking for so little in a potential partner.

Everything was going well until he sent me a photo of his hand (he claimed to have fat fingers) and I spotted a wedding ring. Amateur move. I told him about himself and moved on. Life was too short to share a penis. Even virtually.

So... I kept searching.

Did dude just snooker himself? Surely that's his wedding ring in the shot he sent. Sigh…
#40DayDating #NahFam
#YouNeedToThinkBeforeYouPressSendBruv

Surely there had to be someone out there for me. After Saturday's concert woes, I wasn't really up for any more musical dates. That said, I started talking to a guy who worked backstage setting up massive concert wiring and technical stuff that I refused to understand.

He was from East Africa and lived outside London somewhere but was here for some gigs he was doing. His profile said that he was into F1 and tennis which completely bore me unless a Williams sister was playing but, OK. We didn't have to like the same sports.

We started talking and he said that he hated football. Who hated football? I wasn't sure about him but, he seemed sweet enough, so I decided to go for a Balans-on-High-Street-Kensington date. I could walk there in less than an hour and therefore justify having a dessert. Shame I didn't like any of their new selection of puds. Yes Balans, I have forgiven you for the previous dates at your Westfield Stratford branch. It's not your staff or food's fault. Work on the desserts though, please?

He was running late as he decided to walk to High Street Kensington and, a), didn't really know where it was and, b), didn't understand that nobody walks to High Street Kensington. Too many hills. He got there 30 minutes late when I was already on my starter. Yeah, I'd given up waiting for people. When I'm hungry, I'm hungry.

Straight away I noted how short he was and… his shorts. So only one of us decided to make an effort then? This was a date that was so casual, it was as if we had been hanging for weeks. I didn't need to see ashy shins on date one though. The weird thing was that I'm neither a 'height-ist' nor a fashionista. I just believed that any first date could potentially be your last first date and you should make an attempt to show that you put in some effort. And don't lie about your height, because here he was, considerably shorter than me in my flats. He didn't smell, so he'd managed to have a shower at least, I guess. Yes, I was reaching.

Surprisingly, he was really easy to talk to and we fell into smooth conversation. At one point, I felt that I may have been asking too many questions as he was rather laidback. The good thing was that once we stumbled on a topic that he enjoyed talking about, i.e., himself, we were fine. He told me that he had to flee London in the '90s after his friend stole money from the company that they both worked at and had given him some. So he was a thief? I guess he had spent the last 20 years rebuilding his career and reputation whilst trying to avoid his old company. And no, he hadn't paid the money back.

There were no questions about me. Instead, he chose to tell me about myself. It was now apparent to me that many men thought their opinion of a woman they had just met really mattered. It didn't. He told me that Chelsea was a posh area but then, I was a posh person. We, or rather I, had barely gotten into our main course. Oh, he wasn't eating because he thought Balans was too posh (hardly) and that High Street Kensington was for snobs. Sigh. This was now one of those conversations where you try to tell people it's all a matter of choice and taste and convenience as he was staying in Lancaster Gate. This was the best halfway point between us that I could get to. I didn't want to suggest Bill's in Westfield again. What if he hadn't turned up?

He made some comments about my weight which I won't repeat. Needless to say, I ordered an extra side order of chips to show him that I wasn't going to be shamed into not eating just because he had some hang ups. I reckoned he was worried that he wasn't going to be able to lift me later. I don't know. But we moved away from this subject and onto what I hoped was more neutral territory: Africa.

Alas, he thought it wise to share his nonsensical views on South African history and politics. He had spent three days in Cape Town once, so that made him an expert. This wasn't going well and luckily, I didn't have room for dessert, so we left. I picked up the bill because he refused to eat but then he later told me that he felt bad that he hadn't paid. Seeing as he still hadn't reached into those grubby shorts for his wallet, I'm guessing he was just paying lip service.

As we left Balans, I had a Samantha moment when he tried to hold my hand as we were walking, and I tripped. To be fair, with me towering over him, I felt like his mum.

When I got home, he sent a message to say that he wanted to meet up again as he had had such a good time. Looks like telling me about myself was his idea of fun. I wasn't up for meeting again to be honest. Why? Well his fraud stint in the '90s did no favours for his character, his dissing me did no favours for his likeability and his general demeanour did no favours for… well… anything. To put it simply, we weren't really a match although if I was looking to add more acerbic friends to my circle, he would be high up on the list. However, I do have enough friends like this already, so I didn't think I needed another one.

Perhaps next time don't diss my 'hood, weight or country of origin on the first date then suggest we meet again. This is common sense that anyone can follow.
#40DayDating #Date32 #WhyMeBlackJesu
#NotFirstSecondOrFifthDateConversation

I bumped into Fraud Doesn't Pay months later in Debenhams, Oxford Circus. He was with this white woman who was considerably bigger than I was. He avoided looking my way, so I know he recognised me. He didn't even make 'we're-the-only-two-black-people-in-the-shoe-section' eye contact. I guess weight was no longer an issue for him or he'd decided that lifting weights was his thing. He also didn't pay for anything at the till which showed that at least he was consistent on one thing. Cheapness.

Hey ho! The search continues.

Conversations with Kale Concerns

I'm talking to a guy online and going by his food combos, I don't think we could ever work. I *hate* kale.

How does kale go with mince and pasta? How are you cooking kale like it even tastes nice? It's horrible. How did you spell Jelly Babies wrong twice when I had written it earlier? #40DayDating #IHaveQuestions

Me: You are having kale with mince and pasta? Okaaay… I was starting to worry you thought kale was a food group

Chef Kale: You dissing my food?

Me: I'm about to have a brownie. No, I'm dissing kale.

Chef Kale: I love brownies and Haribo. Cola bottle Haribo.

This user has been deleted.

Date 33: The High but Dry Healer

He appeared, faded out then, a few weeks later popped up again. I guess we were both a bit bored of it all, but I was going to pretend to be less bored.

On paper this one looked perfect. He was French-speaking, good-looking, had a job, an old career in the city and seemed to be saying all the right things which what was needed at that moment. To be honest I think I'd hit another energy slump. It was like all of these guys and not one of them was decent enough to make it to a second date? If I was less cocky, I would start to think the problem was with me but, nah! It was definitely with them. I was still the right side of cocky.

Day 44 and I was starting to get a little suspicious at the level of his perfection. What if he was shorter than he'd said? Or his pictures were really old? Or he was a wanker? But no, I shook away the negativity and told myself that I was just reeling from the disappointing first 50-odd guys I'd interacted with. I took a deep breath and decided that some positive mental 'attituding' was in order. Maybe he was the one? A candle, some sage and a few deep breaths later and I was ready to go again. Ahhhhhh. That's better. I really don't want to take Date 32's energy with me into this one.

#Date33 tonight. He's a healer so let's hope he's not too broken #BlackJesuMakeHimDecent #And Taller #DatingGodsPleaseLiftTheCurse

We agreed to meet at Embankment which was now a regular spot. I hoped none of the station staff thought I was planning anything criminal what with my hanging about then going off with different men each time. OMG did they think I was a middle-class call girl? For some reason this made me smile whilst I was waiting, and he was running late. Yes, here was the first failing. Why has being late become the norm? Grrr.

In the end, he was just 15 minutes late (so practically on time) and we walked over to Giraffe for a drink. He was hot and not short. Winning. But his energy seemed kind of low for a healer/trainer type person. Normally they're like kids on sweets. I wasn't sure. Maybe I was just not his type and he didn't know how to say it.

As the night opened, the truth of it was that he showed himself to be a boring shit and a wanker. Turned out he used to work in the city and despite leaving it all behind (they made him redundant and he'd reinvented himself as a spiritual healer), he still had that city attitude we all know and loathe. I mean, I was just trying to have a conversation, but all he did was spew hate. He hated London, he hated dating, he wanted to move to Paris where he was appreciated… and all this was said with lips that were dry.

This was his biggest sin. Why walk around with dry lips when you were a healer? To get that crackhead shade of white, you really had to have resisted liquids all day long which meant bad breath was likely, ergo no kissing was going to happen. Who went on a date without doing a tube window lip check first?

Date 33 showed promise but dry lips and a banker wanker attitude = 55 minutes of hell. I've had more fun at my gynaecologist. #StruggleIsReal

It was clear to both of us that this wasn't a match. This dude was actually making me look cheerful and bubbly. I hated his miserable and shitty attitude about how life owed him for being amazing. It would never work as we would both want to be the centre of attention and he wouldn't settle for less than 100% of it, and all the time at that too. I could envisage him telling me off for eating in bed or wearing holey socks. In fact, he was so uptight that even the waiters started to act on edge.

Fifty-five minutes later and I couldn't fake it any longer. Dating with dry lips, no sense of humour and a chip on one's shoulder should be date-criminalised. Why was this dude wasting my time? Any initial positivity faded as he sneered at the waitress, the bill (all £7) and at me. I just wanted to be in my bed in peace. So much for being a spiritual healer.

In fact, this was my second healer type and they weren't working for me. Underneath all that artificial zenitude was insecure narcissism. Not for me thanks. *Next*!

Date 34: Septuagenarian

Coaching and matching has left me little to no time for #40DayDating. Still stuck on tricky #Date34. Come on son show yourself (*sans* dick pic).

After High But Dry Healer, I inadvertently took a break from dating. I still did the occasional swiping, but my heart wasn't really in it. Instead I threw myself into coaching and matchmaking. Those who can't, teach, right? I didn't understand why it was taking so long to get the elusive 34th date but by day 57 I had all but resigned myself to just the 33 dates. I'm not going to lie; I began to worry that I was starting to put out the same energy as the healer. That crap is hella infectious.

I did talk to a few new prospective dates, but they were all pissing me off. It sounds strange but I think we were in one of those planet retrograde months where people acted in a strange and inappropriately aggressive way too early. Not the retrograde where your exes come back. The other one. One guy came close to being Date 34 but then he tried it with the 1am text after nothing for over a week? Then dared to play the, 'you're just another angry black woman' card. Fuck him. I love my sleep too much. The search continued.

Then Kathy Bates came back on the scene. Kathy was an almost date, but his English hurt my spirit. Once I discovered that he was a born and bred Londoner, I couldn't accept the poor WhatsApp messages sent at all hours of the day. But then we had a conversation on the phone, and he came across as almost normal. Not completely of this world to be honest, somewhat ethereal, but he came across as having a good heart. Maybe he was an air sign? By this time Facebook Family were well acquainted with Kathy so I let them know that it was finally on.

In other news I'm meant to have #Date34 today with Kathy Bates. Wish me safe travels home. #40DayDating #Final7

Alas, I had to cancel him because *despite* me telling him not to text early as I struggle with sleep, he texts at 5.30am then apologised for texting early? No, my brother. No.

See Exhibit A: I don't get people who can't hear or understand reasonable requests or live on the fringes of life. How are you Tindering hard and yet you don't seem to be able to have a normal phone? How did you even manage to work the app? I can't anymore. I was Tinderised. This was the end for me.

Me: Did you get my messages on Tinder? Hoping to move the location from Balham to Clapham Junction

Me again: *[2.5 hours later]* Hi Kathy. I see you read this message 2.5 hours ago and just haven't bothered to respond so I'm going to assume you're too busy to respond and meet. No worries. Take care

Kathy Bates: It's not that it's my screen. I was expecting you to ring me at 4 PM as I had to connect my phone to my TV so I can read the messages.

Kathy Bates (again): So you want to meet in conjunction

Me: Why would I ring you at 4? Yes at Clapham Junction at 5pm.

Kathy Bates: Because we are meeting at 5. I'm taking my phone off the TV now so I can only get your messages. Text and WhatsApp don't show on my I watch. Send me a text to my number

An hour later

Me: I called. Your line is busy. This is long. Who has a phone that doesn't accept calls? You have my number as it comes up on WhatsApp.

Another hour later

Me: OK so I'm really done now. Going to head into Shoreditch instead. Stay blessed, yeah?

It was getting to the point where I questioned the basic intelligence of the average dater. Did he really think I was that stupid that I didn't realise he was in a situationship and couldn't talk on the phone? That was probably going to slip out after the Mrs had gone to pick up the shopping/kids/pets or was at work? This wasn't me at naïve Date 6. This was a more seasoned dater who could see through the BS. For a second, I almost felt proud of myself as I headed into Shoreditch. I was getting better at this dating malarkey.

Just when I thought things were getting beyond a joke, I bumped into a new neighbour. I'd met him weeks before at a dinner with friends. He'd tried to borrow a book I had but I'd gotten it signed by the author and I never loan out signed books. This was my 'thing'. When you lose a few over the years, you learn. I remembered him well and we laughed about how we kept bumping into each other. It could have been awkward except, it wasn't.

He was living in the neighbourhood temporarily and didn't know many people. So when he suggested dinner, I didn't think anything of it. I mean, the dude was in his grandparental years. I'd just lost my granddad so was feeling particularly family-focused and I also hated to see old people alone. It made me sad.

Eventually he got it together to arrange a time to meet at Sloane Square. I got there at the time said and, he wasn't there. I called him and he was still asleep. I know he was old but, what kind of afternoon nap goes on past 8pm? I was going to go home but he was insistent that he would be there in 20 minutes, so I hung around. You know me and hunger. I needed to eat.

He turned up in Jesus sandals and some crumpled clothes. Sigh. Thank goodness this wasn't a date. We eventually ended up in Pizza Express on the Kings Road which is not my favourite place. Gluten-free pizza base without dairy just makes for dry food but, yes, you guessed it, hungry.

It was a lovely conversation. He told me about his children who were the same age as me, his work as a writer, his travels, etc, and I told him about my life which was mainly concerts, Jelly Babies and dating to be honest.

Then it got weird. He started asking me more personal questions and I tried not to answer them. They were about the dates and ED – erectile dysfunction. How is this normal dinner conversation? How was this a good way to spend a Wednesday evening? Then I thought that maybe he was struggling with ED, so I did try to answer some of his questions. I hated going into coaching mode on a date but clearly, he needed it. I don't understand why he wasn't online 'Viagra-ing' like everyone else.

The bill came and he paid it. I told him no, but he insisted as we finished off our hot drinks. I guess he needed one before bedtime. Then he suggested we go watch porn together at his place. Great way to end the date. A date? How was this a date? *Shit*! I'd been tricked into going on a date. Again.

I had one word. Euuuuw! I mean, old hanging balls aren't sexy. You have to have loved those balls for years. I asked him how old he was and turns out he was in his mid-70s. I just made an excuse and left running.

I now see him all the time and he wants to meet up again. I'm going to have to stop ducking suspiciously behind shop doorways on the Kings Road. It looks… well… suspicious. Despite myself I had to chalk this one up as a date. It hurt my spirit though. And I wince every time I see Jesus sandals now. This was an all-time dating low.

Tonight I dated a septuagenarian. I didn't realise it was a date until he suggested we watch porn together.

Date 35: The Short and Tall

So the mistake that this one made was giving me *way* too many personal details. He was local to me, he owned a restaurant, he gave me his real name and sent me copious photos of him posing unnecessarily. All a bit too pushy. I wasn't feeling it but gave him the benefit of the doubt as I couldn't put my finger on what was bugging me.

He kept mentioning my body which given we hadn't met sent red flags to my brain. I know to some that this makes me sound ungrateful, but I really can't stand those who over-compliment especially on looks. I know I'm average-looking at best and I'm comfortable with that. So, you telling me about my body wasn't going to work. Clearly, he just wanted to shag.

I told him to please cool off on the compliments and he flipped and told me to chill. Huh, I told him that despite us arranging a date, I wasn't going to keep it. I was out.

The dude got abusive and I promptly deleted him. He continued to abuse me, so I blocked him from WhatsApp and Tinder.

Then, a few days later, Facebook did their cookies/we own everything/algorithm thing and suggested him as a friend, and I couldn't resist a wee peek. What he had neglected to tell me with all the other details was that he was married. Married to a woman who was rather tall and, if I'm honest, could take me in a fight. She looked strong but I think I could outrun her. I wouldn't want to risk it, mind. Long legs.

I mentioned him to Facebook Fam and everyone said I should call him out and tell his wife. A whole me? Do I look like I want to die at the hands of a short angry Nigerian guy or a tall Polly? I decided to let it go but kept his texts for 6 months just in case I bumped into him at the local farmers' market.

Lesson learned? Don't give out too many personal details when they live too close and can ruin your life. All he had on me was my favourite dating spot and luckily to date I've never ever seen him there.

PART 11

Dating's Gone Bad

Date 36: Ghana Must Go

#DateDilemmas. I came home and promptly took my bra off. Do I brave braless tonight or would putting my bra back on count as 'making an effort'? #40DayDating #Date36

It was one of those Fridays where I didn't want to do anything. Maybe it was a heady combination of work and dating fatigue but there was sugar and mindless YouTube in my future. Then my daydreaming was interrupted.

I'd been talking to this guy on Tinder who apologised for a two-month disappearance. I hated ghosting but I hadn't been invested so it was not a big deal. Apparently, he wasn't using his phone in Ghana. I have friends in Ghana. Data wasn't an issue. He suggested meeting that night and in a post-sugar moment I said why not. I told him I had tickets to an African night at South Bank which wouldn't be awful… I hoped. I have ticket addiction and always got tickets for something. I only go to about 70% of events though. It's nice to support artists and have last minute options.

He said he was up for it as he really did want to meet. However, I had to confess that I couldn't remember what he looked like. In my defence, it had been two months and nearly 80 men ago. I couldn't remember everyone. Scrolling up, I realised that we'd chatted for less than a week before his disappearing act.

Anyway, he said that he would send me a photo and he did. I was not impressed and my plans for going out waivered. But my best friend had bought me a book about saying yes and I was trying to stay positive even though the dating challenge had me somewhat jaded. It shouldn't be this hard. I kept my bra on. Let me go and do this thing! *[cue some '80s rock theme; I think I was having a Whitesnake 'Here I Go Again' week].*

I met him at my spot on the South Bank. Remember the Builder of Date 16? Could he be another ghoster? Yes, at the Mandela statue. I like to see it as the place for South Africans to meet, but I am always a little sad when people don't know where that is, and I have to explain. But he said he knew it. Things were looking up.

Apparently, he lied as he walked around the Royal Festival Hall, BFI and every building on South Bank for about 25 minutes. I forgot that some men refuse to ask for directions. As he finally made it in the Hall, (I got cold and waited inside) I noticed that he'd lied about a few things. By this time, I was regretting my decision to leave my house but maybe when I see him up closer… hmmm… no.

My date is ten years older than his profile says and still lives with his parents. At 50? He's also not 5'6". He's 5'4" #Date36 #WhyBlackJesu #ThisWillNotEndWell #TheOldTwoInchesLie

We settled in for the show and he said, "You look different from your photos." Was he trying to be a fucking comedian at a comedy show? I asked how and he said my hair. I took out the photo and showed it to him. My hair was in twists there and they were in twists now. I'd not gained or lost any weight in the two months. I looked the same. Unlike most men who are still relying on pre-millennium photos, I updated my photo at least every month to make sure nobody accused me of catfishing. I mansplain this to him as I ask him questions. "I thought you said 5'6" and that you were 40?" That shut him up. I hate liars.

The show was funny. He wasn't. In between comedians, he told me that he still lived at home with his parents and that he had kids but that he didn't get to see them that much because he'd spent the last decade trying to set up a business in Ghana. Huh? You live with your parents at 50? How is this OK when you have dependants? I looked for reasons. A recent divorce perhaps? Nope. They split up over 10 years ago. A business gone bad? No. It hadn't really ever started. So basically, it was just because it was comfortable and worked for you to be an international man of no height or mystery? Bingo!

The lowest point of my date (apart from his height) was when he claimed not to know the first black family on EastEnders. Why are you fronting? We all knew there was such a family. I didn't hear of Michelle Gayle anymore, but we all knew her: Sickle Cell Gary Lloyd, Celestine, Kofi and Clyde. He looked at me like I was crazy. I looked at him like he was lying again. And yet you still live with your parents at 50? I know your mum watches that shit. Fuck out of here.

There was zero chemistry, so I was rather surprised when he offered me a lift home. I'd come to realise however that despite zero chemistry some men will still go for the sex opportunity if they think it's on offer. I wanted to tell him it was not there without raising it directly. Like it was not there, and it won't ever be there. It wasn't his height, belly that's bigger than his mind, lack of hair or lack of respect for time. These things I could overlook as they don't really matter. They're annoyances at best.

It was energy… that was lower than mine. It wasn't spiteful like the healer's, but it was beyond laid back. It's the reason he had been working on a business for over a decade and still hadn't launched it. It was the reason he didn't seem to be that bothered about spending any time with his children. Then it hit me: he was either extremely selfish and immature or depressed. I suspected he was mildly depressed, and you all know that I didn't take on projects.

After the show, needless to say, I got on the bus home. He WhatsApped to tell me that he would like to meet again. What for? I didn't understand the tenacity of men sometimes. Maybe I needed some of that tenacity to get this dating challenge going again? Time would tell.

I got in, whipped off the bra and pulled out the snack box and wondered what Michelle Gayle was up to.

When dude gives you stats on Ghanaian boys' names and you query it because all maths matters and his is dead wrong and you didn't get a D in A Level Maths for nowt and he's pissed because he has a calculator on his phone but doesn't know what the calculation is so now he's sulking but you don't give a fuck because Mrs Stacey would be proud that you finally got something statistical right! #40DayDating #MathsMatters

Almost Dates: The Hot Uber

So on my way to a date I was picked up by what must have been the hottest Uber driver ever. I don't say this lightly. I mean, Uber drivers vary in age, race and size but this one was delicious. And turned out he lived locally. I know my singirls, after the short and the tall married guy fiasco, I shouldn't have been fraternising with locals but what can I say. Hot was hot!

We got to chatting and he asked where I was off to. I told him a Tinder date and shared some of my stories with him. We laughed and got on really well. I wondered why we hadn't connected on Tinder as he was on there as well. Then he dropped the clanger.

We were both outside each other's age ranges. OK OK, he was practically a baby. But you know what I've learned on this dating journey? Matching and sharing for others was just as rewarding as hooking myself up. So I took his details to hook him up with someone else. I wasn't sure who yet but, someone.

Later that night, I went on Facebook and straight away on description alone there were a couple of takers. I was optimistic. But, having been here before, I figured best do my due diligence, so we fell into conversation on WhatsApp. Turns out he just wants to shag.

Again? What is it with these local lads and only trying to get their leg over? Plus he lived with his family. Nah fam. I can't in good faith hook him up when the women I know are looking for long not a leg over with an Uber driver no matter how hot. OK, some of my friends may have been up for it but to be honest he doesn't live locally to any of those friends and I can't guarantee size or performance.

Alas, another one bites the dust. I'm giving up!

Date 37: Mr Lidl

Some guys think you're there to entertain them. How are all your responses LOLs and laughing emojis like this is Comedy Central? Is this code for you've got nothing to say? Nah fam. You're cute but, I'm not the one. #40DayDating

So, Tuesday Taurus contacted me and already it was a bit of a mess. It was his English. I struggled with the randomness of his sentence structures and leaving words out. I asked him if he was from somewhere else or dyslexic and he told me that he was from South London. I asked if it was via another country and he confirmed that no, just South London born and bred. I couldn't argue. We all know that the education system in this country has failed so many but if you really want proof, go onto Tinder. He just LOL'd way too much for me.

A word to the wise. If you are not a great speller or you write phonetically, and you've already arranged a date then stop *all* communication via

WhatsApp. It can only end badly for you. Now I'm having 'dowts'. #40DayDating #TuesdayTaurus

Anyway, we agreed to meet up and as he's a labourer. It was a 5pm date which gave him time to get back to Battersea. We agreed to meet at Revolution. On the day he tried to make out that we were meeting at 6.30 pm. This would mean me going home first and I was already on my way, so I screenshot our conversation which stated 5pm. So of course, 4.30pm he stated that he was running late, and I just rolled my eyes and waited.

Revolution had a private function on (how dare they not tell their regular daters) so I had to wait outside. To be fair, none of my dates had agreed to a Revolution meet. Luckily, it was a glorious September day and I didn't mind basking in the sun even though I was tired. He turned up and we went to a nearby café. He seemed nervous and I suspected that he was somewhere on the spectrum but later I realised it was because he was worried about parking...

He managed to get in a couple of times that he had to park quickly as I was rushing him. Errr, we had plans from over a week ago. Hardly rushing. Aside from that, there were a couple of other conversations that worried me slightly.

Date: I'm actually rather shy.

Me: Really?

Date: Yes, ask my mum. I'm really rather shy.

Me: Shy or an introvert?

Date: Both.

Me: Fair enough. To be fair I'm shy too

Date: No.

Me: No?

Date: No. That's a lie.

Me: ????

He had already decided who and what I was, based on not very much. Whilst I enjoyed my one can of San Pellegrino Limonata which I'd nursed for 45 minutes, I hadn't eaten anything and was getting hangry. This was not great on a date. Then he dropped the Lidl bomb.

Apparently if you park at Lidl in Clapham (I can't tell you about the other Lidls) and don't shop there within an hour you get charged loads. I got it. But why was he taking me to Lidl whilst he did half a food shop which suspiciously looked like breakfast ingredients. Muffins, juice, eggs, milk, onions. I almost told him that I didn't eat onions. Yes, I see you and your wild off-track hinting. Lose the onions.

Disclaimer: I've not been to many Lidls in my life. Maybe just to two of them… twice. I had no idea of the layout. He, on the other hand, was an old hand and was in and out of there in ten minutes. He didn't even need to buy a 5p bag as he balanced everything precariously and professionally in his arms, grabbed his receipt and proudly went to get his car. I wasn't happy about getting into a date's car so told him I would meet him up on Lavender Hill when he had moved his car and we could perhaps go for another drink. I wanted to suggest dinner but was worried that we would end up at KFC. Money wasn't something he wanted to spend, clearly.

Halfway through the date and he takes me to Lidl? This is not a euphemism. This is a supermarket nightmare for me. #40DayDating #Date37 #TuesdayTaurus

As I waited for him, I thought about the date so far. OK so, he was a bit cheap and that didn't work for me. Lidl wasn't only about the free car parking as he ended up buying half a food shop which shockingly cost him less than a fiver. One thing I'd learnt was that when you have widely differing financial philosophies it is unlikely to work.

We met up as he parked his car in a street where you could park for free after 6.30pm and went to a bar on Lavender Hill. I offered to buy a round (mainly so I could throw in food) and he soon perked up. Seemingly he had no issues spending my money as his previous coffee turned into a double brandy and coke. Yes, I side-eyed him too.

It became apparent to me that we weren't a match as our personalities didn't get each other. He also had some unresolved 'ex-wife/mother-of-his-kids' issues which I just didn't have the patience for. How are you bringing up baggage on a first date? Here is an example of the randomness of the conversation:

Date: I'm really into the gym. I feel guilty if I don't go.

Me: I'm medically allergic to gyms to be honest and don't go. It sounds like a chore. It's not for me.

Date: *[Perplexed]* Oh! *[awkward silence]* It's a shame we didn't meet last week when the sun was out.

Me: Why? Would you have worn shorts to show off your gym bod?

Date: Oh no. I don't really like my legs.

Me: *[Stifling a yawn]* So what's your best feature then? *[I've dated gym people before. I know the drill]*

Date: My middle torso.

Me: Middle torso… So what, your upper abdomen?

Date: No *[looks at me like I'm stupid]* My stomach and my chest *[puffs up his likkle chicken chest for me to see]*

Me: So, your whole upper body?

Date: Yes. It's the most defined. What's your best feature?

Me: My shoulders

Date: Give me a shimmy

Me: *[Shimmies]*

[Awkward silence ensues whilst I try not to laugh]

#40DayDating #Date37 #IAmNotWell #INeedToStopPlayingWithThesePeople #IAlsoNeedToLearnHowToShimmyWhilstSeatedInMyWorkBra

So, we could laugh although we weren't laughing at the same things. He wanted to date me exclusively which given the fact that the date was only just alright, surprised me. I think some guys can't be bothered with dating. In his case, I also think he didn't want to spend any money on getting to know me. He showed me photos of his children and, fair play, children aren't cheap but, how is this my problem when I don't have any yet? Answer: it's not.

I only agreed to a second date because he seemed really earnest about us being together and to be perfectly honest, I was beginning to think a second date wasn't on the cards for me so, despite the supermarket scare and cheapness I agreed to meet up again. He suggested a nice fish dinner in Battersea as he obviously hated travelling out of his 'hood. This worked for me though and we confirmed the plans. I was surprised that it was a dinner date to be honest. But then even this seemed to be too much effort for him.

#Date37 aka #TaurusTuesday aka #MrLidl took me for a drink two weeks ago. Then he cancelled last week because of work but tried to do a 'let's keep the evening flexible/tag a Tinder' target move. So, you want to hang out later in case your other date doesn't put out? Dude is a roofer. He finishes when the sun goes to bed. Joker

I knew he wanted to get me over to his with his Lidl muffins and eggs. This assumed I hadn't seen this move before. I had. In addition, I suspected he had another woman on the go and she was in pole position. I'm guessing she was

OK with just a coffee date. I was on the bench. Ole Gunnar Solskjaer, I am not. I don't super sub. I told him no thank you and took my date-prepped self home to make my own fish dinner.

I went home from work and thought to myself would it be petty and evil to go home, change into suspender belt and heels then send a pic to him with a 'Don't work too hard 😜' message?

So now clearly, he'd crashed and burned with his pole position woman and was hoping to rekindle our £3.80 date with a mad dash to Lidl. Nah. He must learn to multitask, write and lyric properly and Tinder tag better

I needed to find me #Date38 *tout suite*! And find a supermarket. There was no food in the house.

Date 38: Mr Manchester United

This one wasn't from Tinder and restored my faith in random fate and chemistry.

I was on my road one night when I saw a guy looking at his phone confused and clearly lost. I asked him if he was indeed lost and he told me where he was trying to go. Straight away I noted the cute Southern African accent. I'm a sucker for Southern African accents. Yes, this was Southern Africa Part 2 which after the Hand(some) Builder aka Date 16 probably wasn't my best move. He told me that he was starting a job at a certain hotel and needed to get there. I told him where it was which wasn't too far past my house and we walked down the road together.

It turned out that he was from Zimbabwe, was over to study an MBA, was going to work part-time as a security guard whilst he studied, and supported

Manchester United. I took out my keys as we approached my door and showed him my ten-year-old Ryan Giggs key ring. He asked for my number as the chemistry was palpable and I thought, *bingo,* this is it. Who the fuck needs Tinder anyway? I'd deleted Bumble weeks ago by this point.

We exchanged numbers and he was a keen Whatsapper which is something that I loved. Turned out that there was a Man United match that weekend, so we agreed to meet up at a pub in Battersea. In the week before the match I learned a lot about him and his hopes and dreams for the future. Some men love to share. For example, he wanted to start a business consulting on Africa. I knew of an event coming up and he asked if I could get him a ticket. Huh? I guess the MBA was expensive, but he lived with his brother so didn't have *that* many bills surely? I knew dating a student would be an adjustment but when dude can't afford £8? I didn't think I was ready for this level of financial regression.

I swallowed my disappointment as the banter was just so good. He did work nights which was interrupting my sleep pattern, but I understood. The life of a night security guard is a lonely one indeed.

Saturday came and I put on a cute red and white dress for the occasion and walked to the Latchmere in Battersea near where he lived. It was a good 30 minutes walk for me, but it was a beautiful day and I was finally feeling optimistic again after Hand(some) Builder. This one had a bit of an office worker's belly, but I loved his smile and his chatter. I couldn't make a judgement on bellies alone. I was housing a whole other person in my buddha belly with an appetite to match that of a teenage gang.

I had booked a table that allowed us to see the screen, so I got there early and sorted it out. I ordered a drink but decided to hold off on food until he arrived. And then I waited. I called him as I knew he didn't know the area well and there was no answer. What the hell was going on? Why were these Southern African guys standing me up after being so full on and keen?

The match started and he still hadn't turned up or answered his phone. This one hadn't blocked me though. I suspected that he had just fallen asleep after his night shift, so I went ahead and ordered but this time just for myself. I'd learnt. The food at the Latchmere was rather good so it wasn't a wasted trip and, the game was good. We won!

So #Date38 is a no show as we go into halftime, but my boys are representing with 4-0. You can't win them all Chelsea, you can't. #40DayDating #UNITED

Five o'clock when the match was well and truly over, he called me and apologised. He'd fallen asleep and, as it was his first week on nights, wasn't used to waking up a few hours earlier to go on dates. I could somewhat sympathise as our late-night calls were messing with my sleep pattern too.

Mr Man Utd came back with a heartfelt apology; I've decided to forgive him. Yes, I know I'm probably softer on him because of his choice in football team and being Southern African. Sigh...
However, his birthday is in two weeks so I'm not going to inform him of said forgiveness until we are clearly out of the birthday zone and I can spend my money on something more appropriate like hotels, fancy dress and sugar.
I'm not trying to be petty. I just am naturally petty. I may even outline my petty plan, so he thinks about what he did every day for the next few weeks. Hehehe. I know. I'm not well. Can we just celebrate my forgiving someone?

We continued to talk on the phone and it became clear that this guy wasn't as 'new' to the game as I'd originally thought. For a start, he was *way* too comfortable with my money and wanted to know about my living situation.

When he realised that I was living solo, he mentioned that any future girlfriend would have to accept his son coming to live with him. That's fine but, why would he be coming to live in my space? We had met once accidentally, and this man was already making plans for my spare room/extra wardrobe? And why would his son be moving over when he was only here to study? Jeez, I realised that I was being groomed.

He also talked about sex too much. Trust me, if I'm saying it then you know that it was overkill. For a start he let slip that he was sleeping with two of his classmates. Secondly, he had a penchant for Asian women and Eastern Europeans. This again? I was clearly neither. Then, during some phone sex lite conversation, he let slip that he liked anal play on him. I thought about all the effort of having to go and buy a harness and strap on and… well we know he wasn't going to contribute. This was going to get expensive.

Then he started asking about us having a threesum. Err, could we have an actual date first please? Like one where we were both in the same place at the same time before we introduced a third person in there. It didn't even have to cost that much! Seriously? I was so done.

Basically, I realised that I couldn't afford to support a man-child student who would likely leave me for whomever once he had gotten himself established in the UK. This dude was looked for a transition target and he thought that he had found it. Plus, he wanted to bang all the women he could. Nah. I wish I could blame it on him being a Libra but, no, he was just an anal-loving dick.

Hmm, I wonder now if the threesum was meant to be two guys plus me and I missed an opportunity? Darn It!

I Don't Do Penpals

Me: I don't do pen pals or just hi

Dude: I hear you … (2 weeks later) Hi, how are you? Just checking in

Me: For what?

Dude: I can't just say hi?

Me: See above

Dude: But … hello

This user has been blocked.

#40DayDating #NotExplaining

Date 39: Black Cabbie

I did really like Black Cabbie and it went on for a while. I think it may have lasted almost a month! I know, right? Writing it, in retrospect, I actually can't remember why we never met up though? Wait, let me go back.

He hit me up on Tinder and we immediately started chatting. He was a self-confessed shorty who had left his job to become a black cabbie. For some reason I admired men who had the tenacity to go out and work for themselves. It was brave. He would never go hungry. I had a friend who was married to a black cabbie. This comforted me as I knew how hard-working they had to be. Maybe this would save me on my Uber bills.

He lived in North London but because of his job, coming down to my ends wasn't the worst thing ever and a couple of times he had drop offs close by. I wasn't one to let you come over before we'd done a public place date first. You dated enough weirdos, you learnt, right? Plus, it took me at least 30 minutes to *faux* tidy and do my hair.

Anyway, our conversations were good. We got on. He'd been in a relationship before and had kids. He'd sent me photos of him, his kids and he just seemed really comfortable in himself. He'd call me as he was driving around and tell me silly stories. He was funny with an edge.

Yes, there were some red flags. Like the time he started swearing at a customer whilst we were on the phone. He was on hands-free and the customer was drunk but all of a sudden, he was effing and blinding like a sailor from the late '70s. I don't know where he'd even picked up that kind of language. It put me off but, I wasn't there so… To clarify, I'm a swearer so it had to be pretty graphic to turn me off. The C word was his favourite. And the F.

Then there was the time he sent me memes of women blow jobbing exhaust pipes. They were in the style of '80s *The Sunday Sport* poor taste but he thought that they were hilarious. OK, so maybe our senses of humour weren't exactly a match.

I told him about the 40-day dating and how exhausting it had all been from the dick pics and abuse to the idiots I'd met who wanted me to pay for their existence. He seemed to suggest on a couple of occasions that I wasn't ready for the kind of relationship he wanted because he was a typical dude who wanted to settle down and not date. He didn't want me to work either. I found this strange as surely two incomes were better than one. On the work thing I am clear: if she wants to work let her work. If she needs to work, then let her work. If she hates work and there are children then, that's work. But like with a woman's body, the work thing should be her choice.

And the one time we were supposed to meet, he bottled it. I think he was projecting a lot of his issues and insecurities onto me, but I was trying really hard not to pop psychoanalyse dates before I met them. This was a new direction for me. I know, my singirls, I didn't think it would last long either. I was now sure that he had an aggressive side to him which was why I didn't go to his place like he'd suggested. I played it off like it was the distance. North London? No thanks fam. We agreed to meet one day, however when I was flat hunting. It made sense as he could pick me up and take me around between the properties although I'd have to sit at the back of the cab. I was looking forward to it. It was a different kind of first date.

Then he fucked it all up. After another conversation about hating dick pics, he sent me two photos of women with their vaginas on show. No warning just *boom*! On my phone in full frontal. I asked him why and he said, "Well they're not dick pics." He became known on my Facebook as the Flange Flasher.

He grew increasingly weird and sexually aggressive. This wasn't working for me and I told him. He pretended that I was too uptight but deep down he knew he was wrong because, just like that we went from messaging and speaking all day every day to driving out of my life for good.

Now, my main worry is that one day he picks me up and I don't realise it until it's too late. This was just a long-winded way of saying that Uber and I won't be breaking up any time soon.

Moreover, this is when I realised that it all had to end. The men I was engaging with were getting more and more abusive and it wasn't worth the stress. I deleted the apps some three months after signing up. It wasn't for everyone. It wasn't for me. I had been defeated by a bunch of strangers who in all honesty had no real interest in dating. They were largely lonely or predatory. It was going to be a long winter after all.

Oh, and I still check out black cabbies before I get in. Just in case!

Date 40: Cracked It!

When a dude tries the 'friendzone slip and slide' by asking you out to discuss work. Work? Must be to talk about his work. The way I hate my actual work and now you're trying to trick me into a work date? Real fuckeries.

Just when I thought I wasn't going to make 40 dates, an old friend popped up. I was pleased as I was tired of apps and online dating. Dates 16 and 38 had both exhausted me as I'd had high hopes for both of them. Could it now be that Date 40 was under my nose this whole time?

When I say an old friend, I mean the friendship not the age. He's a really old friend. Like '90s-friend-old' when we were all 'pretending-to-be-American-and-cool' old friend. I didn't really like meeting with old friends because chances were there was a reason we weren't in communication that much. Thanks to Facebook this had changed, and we are indeed all back in touch.

In this case it was also because he was boring and the reason we were initially friends was no longer a friend of mine – she still owed me £5.70.

Here's the main issue: his lips were painfully dry all the time. I couldn't concentrate on anything he said because I'd feel pain just looking at him. I was tempted to reach over and smother them in oil but, he would see this as a come on. I smiled but not too widely in case he smiled back, and his lips cracked further. How could he not feel it? This was not sexy in case anyone out there was suffering from a similar affliction. Sort it out. Your dating life *will* improve if you do. Was this some *Game of Thrones* chic look that I wasn't getting? Because I truly didn't get it.

I was surprised when he asked me out on a date. He'd told me in the past that he found me too different and direct which suited me just fine, but I guess he was now up for trying new things. I could have said no but I was saying yes to all dates in an attempt to be a little more open to love. Don't judge, my singirls; my mother chanted for me every day and I didn't want her to lose faith… or face. When I say she chanted for me, she chants for grandchildren for herself. Same thing.

So I went. He chose a cheap and cheerful place where to be honest the food was average and the drinks had no taste as they were so watered down. How much ice did you need in a vodka cranberry in London? Not that much! He invited me to order food and I was like, why sure, why not?

He went on and on about his evil ex which was always a red flag and I told him a bit about the American Crackhead just to be competitive in woeful exes. I didn't tell him about the blog. No one needed to know that I could out-ex them on the first date. But I didn't want him to know that this was the first proper date I'd been on in days. I didn't want him to know that this was a pity/practice date, so I gave him good date. I may get bored or lazy later but, I was going to give him great first date.

He then went on to tell me about how all women were X, Y, Z. This was always a soothing way to segue into the flirtatious part of the date I find (insert sarcasm please North American readers). Who ranted about women to a woman and hoped that got her moist? It didn't get me moist. I felt as dry as the chicken I had ordered. As dry as those chapped lips. He could sand down walls with those lips.

Speaking of the food, I didn't choose a starter and I didn't have a dessert so when the bill came through and it was less than £50, I figured we hadn't done too badly. I did the purse reach and he did the, 'shall-I-get-it-or-shall-we-go-halves thing?'

[Scratched record sound]

Excuse me? I gave him the look and he gave me some line about me earning more than him so, yeah. I didn't know that this is how we were doing dates now. You invited me to eat somewhere I didn't want to eat and bored me silly and I *still* have to pay for this shit? How is this a life?

This was the perfect excuse I needed to never see cracked lips again. Needless to say, there was no kiss goodnight! But he called the next day to ask me out again and I had to tell him that I didn't think we had a lot in common. He said that this was sad as I was a good listener. How can you tell a guy you're not talking in case you blurt out how dry his lips are? Surely, he would know this. Sigh...

I'm sending out a quick prayer to the Universe to bring me great things with moist kissable lips!

—♥—

PART 12

And That's Dating!

Three Golden Rules

Everyone has a Cinderella test. Mine is sugar based, i.e., Jelly Babies. Will he choose the right colour (green, orange or yellow) or will he threaten me with a move on a pink, black or red jelly baby? Only time will tell… #40DayDating #LastRoloIsTooRisky #ImagineHeDidntLetMeHaveAllTheTwix

OK so hasn't it been a hell of a dating ride! When I set up this #40DayDating Challenge I thought that I wouldn't get more than ten dates in.

After this initial exhilaration over my dating success (to you, some of my precious American readers please note sarcasm and insert here) I realised that I'd have to work smarter if I was going to meet anyone worthy of taking beyond the #40DayDating threshold into happily ever summer. This wasn't going to be easy. So I sat down on my rest day and focused on what had gone wrong and what had gone well. This was a relatively quick process because there was so little that had gone right so far, meaning that I only needed to focus on the wrong. And there were so many Mr Wrongs for so many good reasons. With that, I decided to set up three golden rules if I was to up my game post 40 dates.

---

1. I will wait no longer than 30 minutes for a date

Oh my days this was a bug bear. I'm only one eighth German and that eighth is punctuality. I'm not built for winter or for British weather in general and am too curvy for jeans and jumpers, so I stick to dresses and leggings. Stop your foolishness. I can't ruin a whole outfit with a heavy winter coat just because I'm anticipating your lateness.

There was the one who was just getting home ten minutes before our date time of 8.30pm meaning he took an hour to join me. Why couldn't he tell me before I'd left my house? He had to wait until 8.20pm? How did he think he was going to meet me on time? Oh, he didn't because he assumed we would both be late. Sigh.

Then there was the Half Pint Hotep who was 84 minutes late for a gig. Luckily, I was warm and listening to good music (thanks Sofar Sounds for your acoustic unsigned artist sessions) but, I didn't get it. The only thing he was bothered about was that I saved him a beer. I think this was code for, I'm not spending a penny.

Then there was Cute Dad who was 30 minutes late because he couldn't find parking at 7pm. In SW London. On a Monday? What a liar.

Finally, and most distressingly because I was actually looking forward to this one, was Hot Gym Dude who, first was 15 minutes late, then was due to arrive in another ten, then 30 minutes later told me he would be another five minutes, before finally arriving 53 minutes late, when I had finally had the sense to leave. By then, not even the promise of those biceps could have kept me on that street a minute longer. Why not just say you couldn't get away from your woman and let it go?

So the waiting rule has now been simplified. First though, I won't meet anyone at a station or on the street. I'm not a prostitute. I will wait 20 minutes max for a date, 30 if cute and have given such good banter that I'm already naming our babies in my head.

Kidding. I chose all of my babies' names 20 years ago.

---

2. I will only pay my share of the bill

Remember when we were in a recession and nobody wanted to put their money on the table? When going to dinner was going to Nando's every single time? When guys used to tell you that they had just eaten whether it was 6, 7, 8, 9 or10pm? Then they looked longingly at your food and stole your chips?

Yes, we were back there again. Which was not a problem. It's good that people are being careful with their money and I don't need a man to splash the cash on me. That said I'm really not ready to splash the cash on them either. I get that they have child support and rent to pay but, so do I. My child support consists of books, clothes and music. Feeding my inner child. Here are some of the all-time best reasons for not paying the bill:

The Cheeky Coffee One – "I know you don't want me to contribute do ya? You've got this. I only had a coffee." ... And half my chips!

The Nando's – "Babe, you got change?"

The Heineken – He who paid nothing but then tried to come home with me but had cab money to get himself home.

And BBZ, the dude who told me that he was trying to save for a property so, err, yeah… money be tight. His bill was £21.

This role reversal thing was not cute, and I've decided that I will make it clear to my date that I'll happily pay for myself and expect the same from them. I'm not here to sponsor people and their lifestyles. In fact, I will get a t-shirt which says, "Nah Fam, I'm not the one!"

---

3. I will trust my gut

It's OK to give the benefit of the doubt but Maxine Saj, my buddha belly is rarely ever wrong about men. Food, not so much but, men? Men she knows.

So why is it that when I can see that they're poor communicators, i.e., outside of reasonably normal hours, are aggressive or use 7-year-old level English, am I still engaging? I no longer have time for this. Yes, the magazines and society have told us to not aim too high because men have the power and choice and are Neanderthals, etc., but this has gotten to a point where basic respect is missing.

So the last and best rule is to trust my gut. It has never ever steered me wrong. Except for that chicken. Why is it always chicken?

OK so, hopefully dating moving forward will be less dramatic. I don't think the wasteman to decent man ratio on Tinder and PoF should be ignored. There are a lot of frogs out there. It's time for me to accept that kissing frogs is not for me. Way too many fuckeries involved.

What Next?

In a nutshell though I realised that for me, the dating recession was real… for now. It had started to change me. I was bored and snapping at strangers because they didn't know how to spell basic words or have an online conversation. Me who spent an unhealthy part of the day on social media and so was used to sassy repartee and *GIF* laughter couldn't comprehend the slow, pedantic ways of the dating app prospects. I say Tinder but I was on Bumble a lot too and that was just as arduous to deal with. I'm impatient and I don't do bored well.

I also learned that most men were on all of the apps and sites for sex. Many to cheat on their current partners and others just to flirt. That was also boring as I turned into the marriage police. I didn't want to not trust everyone there but when so many were lying about basic facts what's the point.

Lessons Learned

This is the hardest bit to write because I feel like whilst I didn't meet anyone with whom I could make a relationship work, I also avoided so many potentially bad or dangerous dates that I'm OK with the outcome. If you look at all the almost dates, there are hardcore, dealbreaker lessons to be learned from this experience...

Online...

...Is not for everyone. Dating apps are a laugh a minute at the beginning but I don't really enjoy being able to judge someone on very little and not having any references. If you are moving around a lot or are new to an area, then dive right in, but if you're stable and have friends then I'm convinced that asking them to hook you up is the best course of action. I encourage more face-to-face dating than swiping.

Men online…

…Lie about a lot of things. Their height, weight, dick size, age, marital status, dating status, who they live with, their children, jobs, education, money and so much more. It's basically a lie festival. They can create the perfect catfish for the rest of us. And all this whilst asking you for more and more indecent photos. The fuckeries.

If you catch him in an obvious lie like age or height, then the chances are he's a mirage who is likely to disappear. How else is he going to merge his 30-something-year-old children with the fact that his profile says he's 45? The only thing for him to do is bow out gracefully to avoid getting caught out. Speaking of bowing out…

Ghosts…

…Love apps and online dating sites. You attempt to meet up and they will stand you up. Then they forget that they ghosted you and try to get back in contact. The problem with ghosting is that there is a risk that you start to think it must be you. It's not you. It's not because you aren't slim, curvy, pretty, exotic, available, serious or adventurous enough. It's because he's a dick who doesn't want to communicate the fact that he's not interested and only here to stroke his ego. Or that he's already in a relationship or married, so this was meant as a means to pass time between shifts. If someone is inconsistent or shady then it's best you leave them alone to sort out their demons.

Safety…

…Is paramount. Early on, I took some risks that with hindsight I shouldn't have. Date 5 Cute Dad drove me home. I would never ever do that again. Best they never have your real number, Facebook profile, name, etc until you are a little more convinced by their online to reality persona. This is for your own good though. And make sure someone knows where you're going and never change location just because the night is going really, really well (by really well I mean he hasn't dropped any political or dating etiquette clangers; harder than one might think). That's what a second date is for, right?

I'm ok…

…with being single. Not forever but, I'm not going to settle for the nonsense goats I've outlined here just to avoid the stigma of single status in my 30s and 40s. People stop asking you, "How are you still single?" and start to ask, "Why?" or "What's wrong with you?" or "You must be broken or damaged somehow." I tend to respond with, "We are all damaged goods but that doesn't mean I'm worth less." I can't wait to meet the man who will be my soulmate and partner in crime but until then I'm happy to drift.

So my experience was fun and I never met my prince but, there are other factors to consider. For one, I have a very low threshold for liars, but the majority of daters seemed to encourage lying to each other until the other person had fallen in love then came the big reveal of the truth. We can't lose hope though. In this same period, I've become a godmother to a bunch of new children so there are relationships out there that are working. Life goes on and so should we. Never give up on what you want for yourself just because you may have to kiss a few frogs first.

But there are good guys out there as well. I even met a few of them and whilst we didn't connect romantically, I could see that they were a decent sort for someone else. Yes, they are a rare find in this fast paced, tech dating world, but they do exist. Hopefully, you and I meet one soon because it's not easy out here on the dating circuit.

And when you do finally meet your person, be kind to them and yourself. Have fun dating and falling in love. It shouldn't feel like a full-time job at the beginning.

Oh! Remember to throw those back who aren't for you. Don't hold onto someone you know is not right for you as a backup. It creates bad dating karma.

Here's hoping its lucky number 41 for me! Or 43... or 44?

Dating in the Time of COVID

It has been some years since the dating apps and now we were hit hard by COVID-19. It would be bizarre to write this book in 2021 and not make mention of a pandemic that's affected every aspect of our lives but most particularly social interactions such as dating.

The subsequent lockdowns have highlighted the isolation of some and given others space to reflect on what they really want in a relationship. Yet others have broken up as the pressure of living under each other became too much. The whole thing has made people prioritise what and who matters and what and who doesn't.

Social distancing meant that dating apps became *the way* to meet new people. People were having video dates on the regular and for some it worked out well. That's right, it hasn't been all bad news for dating. The apps certainly got a lot of traffic especially from men who would normally meet women the old-fashioned way. These were usually the good ones and were snapped up quickly! Whilst most were careful out there, working out who was worth connecting with or not, some people didn't seem to care and created sex and dating bubbles. I hear the number of babies due in 2021 is set to hit the roof due to all the sexual shenanigans in 2020.

So for those of you who are bravely dating during COVID times, I salute you. This is a unique time in our history where chatting incessantly is a core skill for dating survival. I don't have it. I was completely zoom fatigued early from work video calls so the thought of looking cute for video dates *and* having to tidy the flat beforehand was too much for me.

And yet, when I see the love that has poured out during this time it's so clear that human interaction and love are important for our wellbeing. So go out there and love my singirls and singuys. But always, stay sexually and physically safe. Nobody is worth risking your life.

Mwaah x

Thank You

2020 was a difficult year to write. However one of the things I learned was the need to keep laughing and loving. So a thank you to all who made that possible.

My parents and siblings who continuously believe in me.

To my friends who kept me sane during the long writing days and COVID-restricted nights, Samantha, Frances, Erin, Denise, Marie, Natalie, James and Dennis.

To my Facebook Fam because without you this book would not have been written.

Thank you to Danni Blechner of Conscious Dreams Publishing and Rhoda Molife of Molah Media for continuing to work with me in publishing and editing the tricky second book.

All the men who made this book possible. I realise now that you were true to yourselves even when you were lying to me. Thank you. Please, try to be on time.

To my gorgeous godchildren whose antics, videos and pictures keep me smiling.

To all of those precious souls lost to us in 2020. I stopped counting at double figures but family, friends to social media fam, you are all so sorely missed and will be forever loved.

And finally to my future partner. Know that this book outlines the many trials I had to face whilst waiting for you to appear. I *will* bring this up during every argument and when I'm too lazy to get up and get snacks from the kitchen. I love you already.

Chelsea

About the Author

Chelsea Black is a writer, coach and entrepreneur who lives in London. Her current works include her Top 10 Dating and Relationship Blog *The Mizzadventures of Chelsea Black* as well as her first book *Cupid's Cockups*.

She is currently working on a third book whilst listening to music and watching copious box sets under the guise of working from home. She is still actively avoiding the gym, chocolate (some days) and wastemen. Her Soulmate is possibly lost somewhere on the M25 but, will soon be ensconced on their sofa enjoying baked goods and arguing over which boxset to watch next.

Other Books by Chelsea Black

Chelsea Black, one of London's top dating bloggers, is back with more from the world of 21st-century dating. Yes, believe it or not, there's so much more after her debut book *Cupid's Cockups.*

Hitting the dating scene with the same gusto and passion she has for sweets saw her through many misadventures and, she even came out with a serious relationship that nearly saw her move to what was once the land of the brave and the free. (The USA, not a Braveheart's Scotland reference).

But this time, she needs a strategy to find the man who will love the names she's pre-approved for their babies, understands her love of international concerts and can communicate in full text sentences.

Thus begins Chelsea's #40DayDating Challenge to find her prince. Join her as she criss-crosses London for dinners with catfish, ghosts, dudes who claim to eat before the date so that they don't have to pay the bill, yet still eat her chips, and grown men who just can't tell the time.

The question is, will Chelsea find her modern-day prince amongst all the frogs with their fuckeries, or will she have to retreat, re-strategise and hope for third time lucky?

Lightning Source UK Ltd.
Milton Keynes UK
UKHW020024180221
378934UK00014B/954

9 781913 674410